Perhaps

B. A. McRae

© 2018 by B.A. McRae

All rights reserved.

ISBN | 9780692077955

Caution: regarding the blacked-out pages in this book

This book contains raw words and sensitive topics which may not appeal to all audiences.

I am in no way romanticizing such things, nor do I encourage one inflicting harm upon themselves; I simply wish to bring these very real things into the light and spread the awareness of them all.

Because whether we wish to acknowledge them or not, they are here, and I will no longer let them eat away at the beautiful souls they hold captive.

We will no longer look away from these issues and hope they will flee in time, it is time we let it be known that these are our lives, this is our story, and they are not welcome in our next chapter.

These words are for you, whether it is an escape route or a safe haven, this is yours.

And thank you for picking it up.

"Sometimes I see glimpses of the life I saw when I was a child.

That's what I'm looking for,

in this time of darkness, I will find the light of my younger self:

and I will let it run wild."

- B.A. McRae

Yellow Paint

Someone told me a while ago that it was too late for me.

At times I would agree, this isn't what I'd like to see, but this is my reality so gee who am I supposed to be?

I always thought it was polite to be shy and I don't know why; I think someone in my life made me afraid to be myself.

So I would retreat to a secluded seat and stick my soul into movies I could run away through and grand escapes I could only find on the bookshelf.

I don't know what I was looking for, and it appears I haven't found it.

And even though I can't describe it, I just can't quit.

But now I am deciding,

I am no longer looking for a person; I'm in search of a feeling.

And I'm not seeking to unwrap this from a human being, because not all of them are labeled with guarantees.

No, this something is something that is coming from me.

I'm tired of trying to be someone else's favorite when I'm not even my own.

If it takes a lifetime alone to learn to love the flowers my mind has grown, then I'll leave the phone off the hook and listen to the dial tone.

It's not that I don't want anybody; because I believe everybody has that somebody.

But right now, that philosophy is on hold; myself needs me.

For I am exhausted of subconsciously apologizing for my existence by keeping my distance from things that could make me feel different, building myself into nothing.

Though I feel emotionally poor I'm not blind to see I'm not the only one who is in need of something.

This world needs more love.

And believe me, I would love to admit to something else because it's cliché but it's sad in every way that this is the one thing, we're most deprived of.

I don't know how to solve this, but if we all started by trying to love ourselves that'd be something to wager.

Because I swear one day that person, I see every day in the mirror will not be a stranger.

This is the start of the search for a feeling, it almost feels surreal.

All the sudden realizations; I've been borrowing out my smile so long no wonder it doesn't feel real.

The world may not have a clue who I am, and I don't know if it ever will, but I'm not wasting the time I have trying to imprint myself in a stranger's mind.

I've still got pieces of myself to find.

Someone told me a while ago it was too late for me.

Well, won't they be surprised when they see the new spark in my eyes that they can't help but admire, and I can't help to be.

Our Traveler

Souls wander this world wondering what they're all about and what they'll become.

There's a soul that I know, that may not have known everything in the world, but the world was in everything he said and did; he was a person you always wanted to come.

From the moment you met him, you knew he was cool and wondered what a character like him was doing stuck in a little simple town like this.

But he showed how living a life that may have seemed simple was simply extraordinary, thankful for what he had and what he would be; man is he going to forever be missed.

I don't know his regrets; I wish I knew his wishes.

I know his smile and heart will live in the intertwining lives he touched forever, and forever we will see him in the adventures we have and the streaks of sunlight in the sky that soak in our skin, and like his soul in ours enriches.

His voice made you happy, his smile and laugh are contagious.

His words were wise, he'd be the comfort in your cries, but in the end, he was real with you and taught you to be courageous.

His loyal faithfulness ran thick until the end.

He will forever be a most remarkable son, person, and friend.

His footprints will forever embark on the hearts he touched, and the lands he explored.

The nights filled with pizza, card games, poorly budgeted movies, telling funny stories, will remain young and free like he will always be; with him, you just couldn't be bored.

I wasn't the one who knew him best, but he was the best person to teach us what he always preached; life is too short.

Now he's surfing and searching the white waves beyond this life, he'll watch over all of us and wait for us at the port.

He wouldn't want us to be sad, for now it seems to be the only expression, but his blessing in our lives will bring us out of this depression, but without a question-

He is pulling off a hoodie and beanie in Heaven.

In loving memory of Colyn Robert Lauer 08/25/1995- 12/12/2016

Happily Distracted

Her heart was laced with flowers that grew with every enduring beat.

A soul of a dancer with two left feet.

She told me I was silly multiple times a day.

Probably because every time she spoke, she took my breath away, we both usually ended up laughing anyway.

We both loved adventures, but just little things.

Bundled in layers upon layers to stargaze in the winter, going antique hunting in the spring.

Her fingernail polish was always half off, but I never really had the most neatly combed hair.

But I liked the way the colors cracked off her nails, as for my hair she didn't care.

We were too distracted by the company of each other.

She always told me I was the mystery, but I disagree, there's just something about her.

Long ago from learned mistakes I vowed I would never lose myself again.

Though I never completely did I couldn't help it every now and then.

There was a time we giggled and ran out into the night.

No anxiousness, no phones in our pockets; not a cloud in sight.

We ran through the forest without a care, I got lost through the small streaks in her free-flowing hair; flashing me her smile as she turned from behind to me in a quick spin.

Her smile will always be my most precious memory; the moonlight melted on her skin.

We ran out quite a ways then stopped in a clearing to lie on our backs and enjoy the night sky.

After a few minutes of comfortable silence, she turned on her side with glossy eyes and asked me why.

Why I stuck by her side through all her flaws and such.

As I was about to correct her, my hand she clutched.

She really didn't know why I loved her so much.

So with her hand in mine, I told her "I don't love you to the moon and back; my love for you will reach and ricochet off all the stars God ever touched."

"Forever is nothing compared to the feeling you give me; you are my sunshine through any kind of weather."

"And when we grow old and have said goodbye to the world, my beautiful girl, our skeletons will crisp through the decades together."

I held her hand to my lips and kissed her fingertips gently.

Her glossy eyes began to fade; her smile came back to me.

Now I call her silly, but she gives it right back to me; life with our small adventures was nothing short of peaceful.

A flower laced girl and a messy-haired boy; just two happily distracted people.

The Skyline Room

The room looked like the world inside of it froze in the forties.

Within its old but timeless interior held one of my favorite stories.

Darling do you remember me when I was twenty, hardly had ten dollars on me, yet my eyes were set on the most expensive thing in the room; and it wasn't any man's pocket watch or a woman's dress.

It was your eyes and their disguise that you were utterly bored of this party but couldn't confess; it was you who was priceless.

I came with a buddy of mine who was in my unit and we both had the objective at the end of the night to not be sober.

For September of '45, I couldn't have been more alive; the war was over.

The room wasn't too shabby, not that it would matter if it was falling apart because for tonight right now the world wasn't falling apart, everyone was happy.

My pal had his eyes on his drink, as for me now I couldn't even think; I exchanged my gin for water, tried to stand a little taller and hoped you were free.

The space we were in wasn't all that big, it was dimly lit, smoky quite a bit, and the skyline of New York City was painted on the back wall.

You were leaned against the city that never sleeps, watching the dancing and singing of awakened souls, but I couldn't see them at all.

You may have been trying to blend in with that black dress of yours but within the smoky and noisy essence of the room you were glowing.

And within me it was clear and quiet as the intense desire to talk to you, even if it was just for a minute, was growing.

Maybe it's bold to say but believe me on that day I wanted more than anything to be your groom.

I swear to you and anyone who will listen that I was captured in your eyes glisten; I fell in love with you that night in the Skyline Room.

I won't lie when I say I was surprised when you first smiled to me.

And in your arms during our first dance was my new favorite place to be.

We were the last ones to leave.

Your pinned-up hair and my rolled-up sleeves.

Even when everyone left, and no music was playing we were swaying.

Slowly our feet moved but my mind was racing.

I whispered something in your ear and had I known what you'd do after I would have said it sooner.

You kissed me on the cheek, and we danced closer.

Darling I'm not, we're not twenty anymore.

But as I return to this room I feel as though it is again my first time walking through this door.

I look over to the skyline and imagine you standing there.

You with your mystery and wavy hair.

I wouldn't have guessed I'd be so blessed months down the road you'd say yes to me, and after 50 years of marriage, you'd still make me feel the love we had felt when we were young.

And if you were here, we'd celebrate the big 51.

But I can see it in my head, and I can feel it in my soul you're with me right now.

As I stand in the room that hasn't changed, not one thing rearranged, I reached my hand out remembering our vows.

I will love you and only you even when I can't see your face every day.

I will be with you and only you even when you can't find anything to say.

For the people walking by, let them stare at the funny poor old guy whose dancing with his hands holding nothing but a dream.

I don't care because they're not aware that we're back in that moment, that perfect moment when I knew I wanted to be yours; it seems we fit with the room's theme.

We're twirling about the floor, there isn't anything I want more, I'm envisioning your smile as I whisper to the air what I whispered to you all those years ago that I'll always remember.

I'll never grow old in September.

she was my Breakfast
                              in bed

And I her
         evening
                tea

De Artiest

This is Art, which even at her young age she found it to be ironic.

For she didn't feel like art, she just felt a little lost even at a child's cost, but the world around her wasn't very sympathetic.

Her hero was Vincent Van Gogh because he seemed to be the only one to know the beauty flowers bring.

Flowers, flowers were her thing.

She talked to him, I suppose like an imaginary friend, whether she spoke up to the sky or the space around her, over anyone to talk to its him she'd prefer.

She'd read her Van Gogh books out loud or perhaps talk about her daisy's progress that lives in the front yard, and sometimes she'd pretend that he noticed no one pays attention to her.

No one ever did, for a while she got used to it, but now she was through with it.

Throwing on her raincoat that fit a bit too large, she cut through the garage, making her way to the front yard where she scooped up some dirt and her daisy and nicely placed it in her deep raincoat pocket.

A small backpack on her shoulders that held all her Van Gogh books,

She walked the memorized path, not too concerned about the town people's looks.

There waiting for her was a canoe, she always loved canoes.

It was off a beaten path, almost like a community canoe, she picked some flowers on the way and along the bay, placed them in and took off with nothing to lose, a little water in her shoes.

Physically she was alone, but she didn't feel like she was by herself.

For all her friends were here, her flowers, Vincent, all her books off the shelf.

She used to cry a lot, she doesn't like to anymore.

Eventually, she'll have to go back but there's just so much sky to explore.

As she got to the middle of the water, she gently placed the daisy and the handful of dirt on the wooden bench in front of her and smiled; she laid down on her back and watched the sky.

Imagining her old friend painting his colors across the blue canvas; taking away her anxiousness and releasing a sigh.

Born into loneliness she doesn't deserve.

Waiting for a love that shouldn't be on reserve.

For she is far too young to bear such pain.

Maybe that's why she wears her coat, so she's always prepared for rain.

Comfy

He: We met at the Discount Donut Shop, and I think it's the most adorable thing ever.

He: She probably secretly wishes we met in some romantic movie scenario, but we have each other so it's whatever.

She: I think when we met, we were reaching for the same donut and I gave him a look so that he very well knew that donut would be mine.

She: And what do you know I got the donut and a pretty cool guy who shares my time.

He: We'd drive around on my moped.

She: He was a dork for the color red and bread.

He: Yes, I have a moped, and yes, she thinks its super cool.

She: We'd drive around the boring town and find something to do; like our own little nerdy carpool.

She: But tonight, we're staying in because it's raining.

He: I love when I catch her singing.

He: "I'm pretty sure it's my night to pick the documentary!"

She: "Nope I'm pretty sure it's not, you picked that one about the monkeys."

He: "It was worth a shot, hey wanna order pizza, I'm about to roll down hunger hill."

She: "You're gonna make that poor pizza person go through this rain, although pizza sounds really good; Hun have you seen the candles?"

He: "We can convince them to quit their job and watch TV, or maybe us three will make our very own documentary; just kidding, I'm ordering, and I believe they are in the bottom drawer my love."

She: "Ah yes, a classic documentary of a time lapse of three couch potatoes; can we please get pepperoni, and I found them they were in the drawer above!"

He: She loves any excuse to set out candles, and I love any excuse to be with her.

She: Candles lit, a nice documentary, a comfy place to sit; and with him beside me, eating pizza, there's no other place I'd prefer.

He: Her lips were always slightly chapped; she would never admit she was actually cold but still my sweaters she steals.

She: There was always just a little bit of dirt lingering under his shortly cut fingernails.

She: And I wouldn't trade him for anything whatsoever.

He: I dare say she is my forever.

He: We had a highlighted TV schedule cut out from the newspaper hanging on the fridge like a couple of old people, these are the little things that make me giddy, and I couldn't imagine myself with someone else, no one else could make me this happy.

She: He wanted waffles for every meal, and he's never seen the sea, but he said it can't be much prettier than me.

She: He's definitely, and thankfully, not like other men.

He: She was the kind of girl who was daring enough to always do a crossword puzzle with a pen.

She: He's my spinning top that will never rest.

He: She is my Sunday best.

She: I could feel him looking at me "Hey, you're missing the documentary."

He: "I'm looking at one; it's called 'The Definition of Beauty'."

She: "Oh stop, you dork, you always make me blush."

He: I don't think I'll ever lose this feeling; she'll always be my crush.

He: She's my ladybug.

She: He's my hot chocolate in a Christmas mug.

He: "Hey Darling, can I tell you something?"

She: "Why of course, anything."

He: "I love you."

She: "Aww Honey I love you too!"

He: "Aww really really?"

She: "Yes silly, now shh, eat your pizza and watch this documentary."

Ninety-Nine

I've spent a fair amount of time at the bottom of my shower.

Shower floor?

Shower ground?

Whatever it is, it really doesn't matter now, now that the droplets of water that surround me are sweeping me away with their own rhythmic sound.

Sometimes I just look at my reflection in the foggy faucet until my hands and feet no longer look like mine.

Like I had spent a lifetime away just looking at the misty silver as if I was waiting for it to have something to say, and as it may have cleared its throat, I'm already ninety-nine.

To stand up takes too much energy.

Which sad enough has not been a luxury to me.

Speaking of which, a lot of things have changed.

How I would give most anything for my thoughts to be exchanged.

Most?

That's pretty generous of someone who has nothing even close to be able to boast.

My reflection can't help me escape, it's practically useless.

It has taken such an awful shape; this has become such a mess.

Is this really what people see?

Has this intoxicating poison been leaked from me?

But I can't hear the reason in my thoughts, my words, anymore; everything I do is glazed in an unwanted daze.

Permanent perhaps, alas my delayed ways I have recently portrayed have gotten me the opposite of praise.

So here I am; screaming to get out, clawing at the inside of my scalp.

The scary thoughts, the unspoken words collect under my nails as I scrap away begging for help.

The pleads echo into the dark, my only company.

Aching from the scratching, the yelling, who am I kidding; what has happened to me?

Who have I become, when did I fall behind?

Time has become my chains; my only distraction is my pain; sorrow is life's refrain when you're a prisoner in your own mind.

The View from the Moon

He was an odd one, course I suppose I'm more of the odd one seeing I fell for him.

Oddly of all places in a sea of faces, he saw mine amongst life's fast-moving paces, the light upright in the dim.

On a random day, I was at the beach though I don't like to swim.

Later I learned he decided to go on a random whim.

With my book in hand and my feet hot against the sand I barely had the motivation to stand, my intentions were to finish reading these last couple chapters.

His intentions were naive, but with the glance his eyes gave me it made me believe I could sprint if I wanted to, from that day through it was the world accompanied by us two; looking back on it now, it's been quite a few years.

After a while of being together I remember him telling me while getting my attention by gently touching my knee.

"Darling I will occupy your side forever, however, I am sorry to inform you that it will not be too easy to get rid of me."

Boredom never seemed to seep too deep inside of us, it never really had much of a chance; with this guy around it was an obstacle.

For he loved doing many peculiar things, but he loved to playfully tease me with the impossible.

These mostly appeared when inside it felt my mind needed to be cleared, somehow, he could always tell when I needed a break from reality.

Silly things that made me grin like "You'll be the dish to my spoon, we'll run away and be free!"

He'd compliment me in his own weird special way, every day; it was never a matter of where or when.

They filled me up with so much giddiness, even though some of them made absolutely no sense, for instance, one of my favorites: "Opel Looks like the stars are tangled in your hair again!"

We'd fill our empty days with lovely walks filled with deep meaningful life talks leading to a picnic with sandwiches and fruit we handpicked.

We have had many of those, but neither of us would have guessed or known in his odd internal arithmetic he'd miscount the days we had left before he got sick.

He insisted the walks and our routines persisted, and it did as long as we could.

Through the piles of bills, I tried to keep from him and trying to distract him from his quickly slim looking limbs, still, he gave me those eyes that came with matching sayings that still made me feel good.

"I'll wrap you in the Northern Lights and hold you tight while we travel through time and space until we find February 30th in the perfect place."

I did my best to make him feel he was still independent, there were things we had to give up to pay for the hospital bills and rent, but we were always still happily content; but some days it pained me to see him so weak, at times I hardly recognized his face.

But the touch of his hand will always pull me back to the sand on that destined random day on the beach.

And when he'd stroke my hand with his thumb, I swear I could almost hear that undertone-busy-beach hum; the sky was painted blue with the most delicate sprinkle of peach.

In the midst of the stressed-out look, I unconsciously always had on my face he'd pull me into his loving words again.

"I'll plant a breed of a whole new species of trees on Neptune for you because I know you love the color blue; I'll make you a suit to sustain the cold and you can run through the trees without any tension or ease, just nice and open."

Before I met him, I didn't like being out and about, I kept to myself because, well that's what felt safe; I could escape through my books without a single trace.

And now here I am caught in the eyes of this guy who says things like "I'll hang a swing from the moon just for you, because I know how much you don't like people and you love the feeling of space."

I haven't read in a while; I haven't had much time for it, and I feel bad because he feels guilty for seeing it.

"I'll make a newspaper for you for every day, delivered with freshly made lemon bars made by a little old baker who tells me the same joke every time I come in, but this paper will only contain the very best comics."

Others close to me hear his little corny testimonies and warn me it isn't something I should encourage or pursue.

They don't understand what I hear from my beloved Dear; for though I know they are things he cannot physically do his passion and love within them is true.

Our empty days are occupied with a bland hospital room we've tried to make feel more like home with pictures and quilted blankets; alas it feels unfeasible to be released from this feeling.

A feeling that our walks may not proceed out those doors again, that we've had our last picnic; I try to mask this all, he has no trouble at all smiling.

Though reading to him at his bedside subsides our lost time, these words of adventure that leaves my lips may captivate his, but they cannot linger long enough in my thoughts that are consumed in the fact that he is getting so much thinner.

His hand touches mine; I hadn't noticed I stopped reading; "I'll send a telegram to all your favorite fictional characters to set up a wonderful day-long dinner."

Could his fate have been different if he hadn't met me?

If I found this was true, that this sickness wouldn't have tangled in him if I wasn't reading and I loved to swim on that random day on the beach, to save him or even give him more time, in the end, I would have lost myself in the sea.

This was our lives, our internal clocks ticking louder as they swung.

How I would give anything to bring us back to when we were young.

When I thought he was asleep I couldn't help my soft weeps at the thought of losing my love, my best friend; I'd cover my eyes trying to hide these quiet cries.

My attempts were never met, he'd hold me while my sorrows I'd try to forget; "I'll bring you back in time and cover your eyes to unveil to you a time where you can experience seeing colors for the very first time and it'll blow your mind." He softly wiped my eyes.

We both managed to comfortably fit in his hospital bed, in moments it even felt like home, the smells of shots and test tubes were suddenly sublime.

His hand caressing my cheek, the other wrapped in mine; "The world will freeze at the snap of my fingers and we shall dance about the entire planet amongst one moment in time."

His hand clenched tighter, his fingers began to slowly slide down my face as he whispered gently "Forever, by your side I'll be, I love you."

These are his last words I carry, his last breath he drew.

I cannot escape from this reality anymore.

I don't know why I always thought for some reason morality would never approach your door.

Darling, you're out of my reach.

Please tell me you'll take us back to our random day on the beach.

Reading is no longer pleasing, there's hardly anything I enjoy to do.

My intentions were to finish living these last couple chapters with you.

Indeed, we were an odd pair who didn't care that we had even odds at a sad ending like any other couple.

It wasn't a problem until it took him, now life is just unbearable.

In my aching moments of solitude, I don't mean to sound rude, but selfishly I take back what I said; I'd pick a lifetime of meeting him at the beach over anything, it's just a nice thought in which I try not to get too comfortable.

I guess he really did tease me with the impossible.

Duende

There's a woman who lives in room 208 at the Aeonian Home with a perfect view of the lake.

She wasn't bitter or mean but by the other residents she was hardly seen; social events she didn't particularly partake.

The world couldn't keep up or wouldn't slow down for the little old woman and her terribly confused mind.

For she firmly believed something a little out of tune; though the nurses were kind, to the situation it was as if they were blind.

There's an easel in front of her window, she doesn't call herself a widow, she is ecstatic to look at it every morning.

Because while she is sleeping, though she is tired of dreaming; she believes her love has left her a painting.

Yes, you heard correctly, every morning she wakes up to find a beautiful painting waiting to be viewed, and along with it each time is the same little note always with the same two words; she has kept each one in a shoebox under her bed.

The nurses help her hang up the paintings, some stay in her closet, or on occasion she gives some of the old ones away to other residents; the artwork of her love she loves to spread.

Her love was a painter, but of course, and they met in Spain where she was traveling, and he was subconsciously patiently waiting for the love of his life to come wandering through.

In no time at all love covered them whole, and later on they became three instead of two.

Their lives were lived through happy memories, a few scrapped knees, but love was always present no matter what.

Love can fill each crack of your soul with the glue it needs, but it also has the strength to pull and twist your gut.

He always figured she'd go before him, there's no preparation in dying.

He left on a Sunday morning without a warning, and a few unfinished paintings.

The devastation made a creation; her imagination became her distorted reality but, in its irony, it kept her sanity, in her world her love never lost their breath.

They never handed in their paintbrush to the cold hand of death.

But of course, her view sadly isn't true.

But if not, her love who brings her paintings and notes, then who?

These paintings are her loves, the ones they've painted throughout all their years; and though she thinks she gives them away they are simply just returned.

Each time she sees one it's like the first time, but by morning with the new paintings it's like the memory is burned.

The narrator and deliver are the same, just as the two words on each note are the same; '*Remember Me*', the words are a hope that someday they'll get to her.

She lives to see these paintings, and I am the son she doesn't remember.

The Colorful Candle

My hands ever so lightly embraced her beyond gorgeous face, my eyes traced her every feature; my eyes were lost in her beauty as her mind was lost in an unwritten future.

She wasn't insecure of my deep love for her, nor did she see it necessary for me to constantly reassure her.

But I knew the way her thoughts trailed throughout her mind.

Maybe she just didn't want me to see that raw part of her, call her stubborn, say she's unstable, but she's more than what she leaves on the welcome mat and sets out on the table; she's mine and I'll be here until and after her thoughts are kind.

There are times she feels as though she's draining the light from me because of my devoted search to find her, her happy.

What she doesn't know, mostly because I don't let it show, is if anything she's pouring the light in and fixing me.

She's so fragile and scared, as if I'm packed up and prepared to leave when things get rocky or she's sad.

Unless she ate my takeout leftovers without swinging it past me, I would never be mad.

She wrapped her hands around mine like she was viewing a snow globe in an expensive store.

I loved her touch so much, and her eyes held a pulling attention I could never ignore.

"Please save me from this mess, please I promise I'll help once I get back on my feet, I just need a refuge, somewhere I can collect myself again and push away these thoughts that scream to me defeat, I'm sorry I'm like this I just don't know what to do" Her words sounded like they were getting caught.

Please don't let go of my hands, I thought.

My arms reached gently for her frail soul, if only she could know how much I wish I could give her more than a promise to show her I will never leave her side.

As I held her close, and I heard the sniffles from her nose I thought of her colors inside her she hides.

She doesn't like them.

I don't know what she sees in my colorful mayhem.

I want her to be able to completely let go because I will be right here to catch her; this fear of hers I will make smaller.

She will melt into me as I to her, my colors will run through as they mix together; our souls on a mission to discover a new color.

Glass in the Sand

How did it become of this; I just barely blinked my eyes.

There's a ringing in my ears, and I can't understand why.

I can't come to grips with the right side of my bed, our bed, being cold.

There's no way I could ever lie in the middle, I left so many things on reserve for when we were old.

Truth be told I can't hold myself together anymore.

I'm broken every which way, I want to leave and go away, but I stay every day; I use to tell myself I do it for you but it's beginning to lose meaning, what do I do it for?

Every day, I talk to you.

The words mock within the unoccupied air, they slip right through.

Your hourglass has broken my Dear.

But still, I still feel you here.

I will still dance in your sand; your footprints appear sometimes with mine.

It may hurt when I step on the glass, but it's worth it, especially when our footprints align.

I notice when your footprints leave though, you have a knack for not saying goodbye; I at least hope you watch me dance alone.

This has just turned into a place; it's no longer a home.

Save me, Dear make me alive again because I have felt so dead; since your feet crossed over the threshold, my life began to fold.

My last morning with you, if only I knew, what life's plot for the day foretold.

I wouldn't have let you get out of bed; I would have held you forever.

Truly you find the source of your light when you lose your treasure.

These bags under my eyes will never fade, because I will always be exhausted from this strife.

I will always be exhausted of life.

Please, if the world is listening give me something; I can't handle the silence, my eyes constantly and desperately roam.

Please, give me back my home.

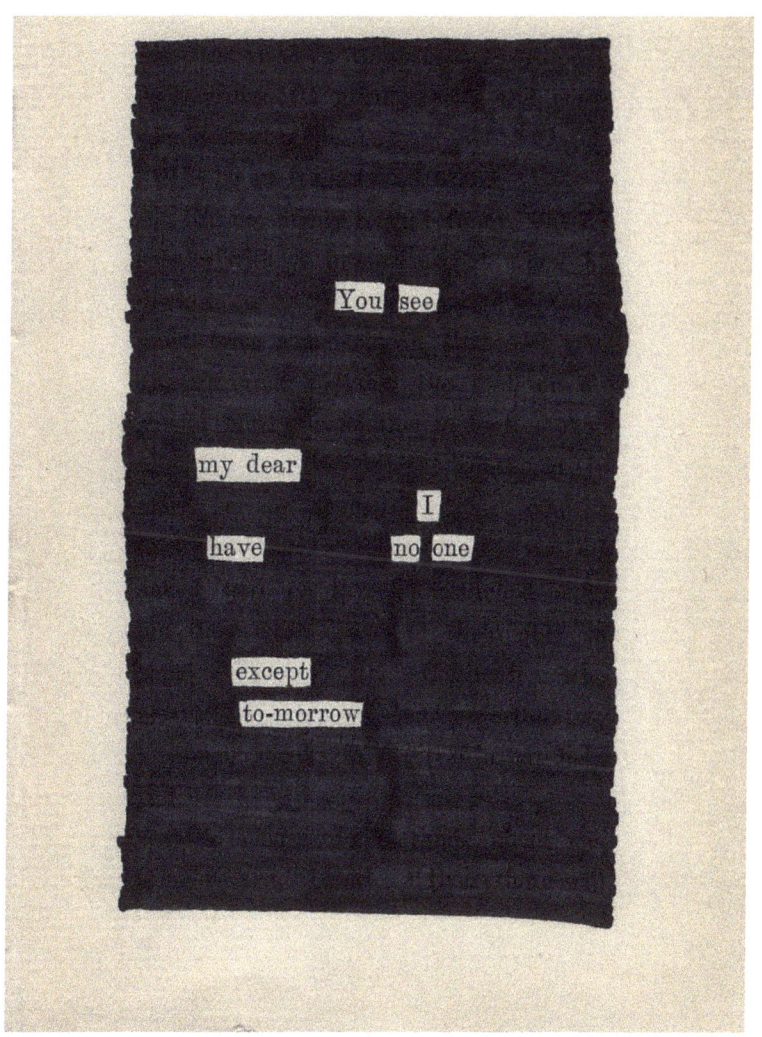

"You see my dear; I have no one except tomorrow"

The Lucky Ones

He was the spark that lit my life, the only man I truly loved.

I had made many mistakes and had burdens I couldn't shake away, but still he held me high as if I were something as flawless and magnificent as a dove.

He knew exactly when I was at the peak of my breaking point.

And each time in our forty years of marriage, he would take me to our favorite pizza joint.

We would walk into the dim lit restaurant, with the sound of pool balls clacking against each other, and the records shifting in the jukebox, as we made way for our table.

Everyone knew when we came in that's where we went, a table set for two right by the window, with the view of the beautiful lake, led by a path of shiny pebbles.

"Tell me Emmylou, do you remember when I first took you here?" he would ask as we took our seats.

I would smile and reply "Yes Dear, you finally got the nerve to ask me when we took a walk down the street."

And we ordered our pizza, while reminiscing our younger years.

I always found myself falling in love with him all over again as he did with me despite our fights and tears.

How could I deserve something so amazing, something only few people are fortunate to possess?

Halfway through our meal he motioned me to get up with him, leaving a tip on the table for our mess.

He slipped his hand in mine and led me outside.

And as soon as we were out the door it was though he transformed into a teenager again, walking with so much pride.

By surprise he began to skip down the pebbled path, bragging me along.

Laughing and catching up to him, I heard softly under my laughter and breathing, a quiet song.

We stopped along the shoreline, taking off our shoes, as he then asked me for a dance.

He put his hands on my hips as I put my arms over his shoulders, in this moment I swore I saw him as I did my first glance.

I laid my head on his chest; his chin lay gently on the top of my head.

He began to softly sing the little song he wrote and sang to me, during the first dance we had after we wed.

"Through the rain and through the shine, my Dear there won't be a time."

"Where I will not be in your heart, for you will always be in mine."

"Life may get scary, and we'll get the feeling that we want to be done."

"But my Love when this occurs, remember, we are the lucky ones."

Decent

The house I grew up in was decent.

Decent became the foundation of my life, after a while I didn't even totally know what it meant.

I lost track of a lot of things.

I didn't have a lot of things, but that's not the point I'm trying to bring.

What I'm trying to say is I've been trying too long.

Longer than I thought I would be, I don't even know me, but I know I'm not that strong.

At least not as high as the people around me set it to be, I'm afraid of this emotional height.

A height that you can't sight until you're at the top and you can't stop looking down, and you want to turn around because you're too tired to fight.

So eventually you stop looking around for someone to come save you.

Because no one knows you need saving, you haven't told a soul so why would they know, technically there's no saving to do.

Sleep ironically becomes a dream.

Hopeful thoughts become a hopeless scheme.

Every latching bad feeling you've acquired,

Mends itself into the easiest response to the simplest question you always get asked "I'm okay, just tired."

Tired and decent turn into an identical mold.

That you don't even realize you pour into every night until it has you in its comforting hold.

After so much time, it doesn't seem so bad.

And this is where you are, and it's all you've ever had.

I don't know where my home is anymore, or how to build a new foundation.

I don't know my place in this faceless formation.

I can't handle the thought that maybe I just don't have a plot, maybe this was an accident.

Maybe I'm just on an endless journey to find a better decent.

Indian Summer

He loved to photograph the oddest things.

Beautifully captured moments, for intense, like my free-flowing hair while gliding on the swings.

The camera always hung from his neck, always ready to capture the world's finest moments away.

It didn't even stop him on our wedding day.

Right when I said 'I Do' he snapped a picture, and the crowd began to laugh.

In the midst of their laughter, I saw our next fifty years in the glisten of his eyes; we even hung up that photograph.

But when we first met, we met in such a peculiar way on an unusual day.

We met at the park while viewing community art; the same one caught our eye, and to our amazement it started to snow in the middle of May.

People thought we were nice, but that we wouldn't last.

And as our time together grew, it was a bet they lost.

Sometimes time moved too quickly for us both, he had drawers filled with small canisters containing undeveloped film; he caught it all.

Someday we would print off all our precious forgotten adventures and hang them on the wall.

We weren't perfect of course; we had our arguments.

Our fair share of flawed moments.

Both of us had our quirks.

To one another they were original perks.

There was a time he smoked from a pipe once, and then he wouldn't stop quoting old black and white movies.

As for me, too often in the middle of the night I would make cookies.

We made our own quirks together though.

Owning too many candles and watching too many shows.

Hiding paper notes to each other.

Playfully throwing freshly printed Polaroid pictures at one another.

For hours on end, we'd play *Nintendo*.

Though he's always been there, I'm afraid one day he'll let go.

He's my special tape I never want to stop playing; I never want it to fade.

Luckily, he's told me he would never leave this amazing life we made.

Life with him was like living through a view master.

I never knew what was coming next, but with each picture it got better.

It made me smile that he never got tired of taking photos of me, out of everything in our surroundings.

Like I said, he loved to photograph the oddest things.

Hollow

She loved the feeling of running her hand along a brick wall.

I loved holding her hands; in mine they were so small.

She, for whatever reason, loved filling ice trays.

I loved how she unconsciously filled me with this warm feeling after seeing the way her hair lays on our lazy days.

She without a doubt figured me out the moment she laid eyes on me.

I won't lie I was surprised how long I got to hold something so beautifully free.

I called her home, she called me boring.

She wanted more, and I had nothing.

Her echoing footsteps wander through the halls of my heart.

Maybe we just need some time apart.

Getting through each day feels like trying to run under water.

Some days the waves hit harder, sometimes I struggle to remember I am stronger; I just miss her.

And is that so bad to say?

Of course, my heart does feel broken, but I wish the best for her anyway.

One day she may come back, and if not then that's that.

But oh, how I'd give anything to have another tired out of our minds, mind-bending, three A.M. chat.

I hope her favorite TV show never ends.

I've composed so many messages, but I never hit send.

I don't want to change anything in case she comes back to me, that way we can pick up where we left off like nothing happened, she just misplaced her key.

I'll trudge through the waves every day; I'll leave the ice tray empty.

Filling my Lungs

I was in the subway,

As I am at this particular time every day.

After some time of this routine, I have recognized some regular faces.

It's odd to see them every day and never meet their acquaintance but know of their designated places.

But there was one person with whom I've made an unconscious daily ritual.

We would always just happen to catch one another's eyes in the midst of our daydreaming gazes and smile to each other; at times it brightened my day even if it is so simple.

I never imagined ever striking up a conversation with them or even thought about the sound of their voice.

In a way I didn't want to hear what they sounded like, the mystery would remain, this innocent smiling game; I'm much too shy anyway if for some reason they wanted to talk it would be their choice.

There I stood in the cold underground staring off into space with my hands in my pockets and my mind in an aimless wander.

I believe my unspoken acquaintance was near, but that left my mind as I began to hear something that sounded like rushing water.

That didn't make sense though, I didn't turn my head.

Moments later in reaction to the screams I heard I jerked my body to the crying words as I saw water pouring in rapidly down the stairs up ahead.

"There's no way out!" I heard in a shout.

Even at the sight my fists were clenched tight, but still my mind had the audacity to doubt.

People were running frantic; I was frozen in my place.

A place I stood every day and up until now I was always okay; the water is coming so rapidly, everything is happening so quickly I don't know what's wrong with me I can't even move my face.

Finally, I got my body to pivot just a bit.

There was no stopping this oncoming flood and here I am like a lousy useless stick in the mud, my mind still couldn't admit maybe this is it.

The coldness of the water just started to hit me; I hadn't noticed it was well passed my hem.

So many people yelling, some running, crying, standing, praying; another thing I hadn't noticed was my acquaintance was looking at me, and I was looking at them.

We were standing just a few feet apart.

I wouldn't have guessed that such a guest in my life would be casted into such a part.

Boldly they stepped closer to me.

As smoothly as they could through this abruptly placed sea.

Though it is extremely inappropriate in this situation and unusual,

We both kept our daily smiling ritual.

It of course wasn't a happy smile; we weren't some deranged psychopaths who were completely ignoring what was going on.

I think we both felt some sort of safety in the smile's familiarity, and with the crowdedness of the subway and this high rising bay, I think sadly quite quickly our hope had gone.

I didn't even know them; I don't want it to end like this.

I don't want the last thing I feel to be wet and out of breath, I've barely had a moment to remember the things I'll miss.

Am I crying, I can't tell?

If I could speak my mind right now, I don't think I'd even yell.

The subway is flooding, from what I have no idea, and for some reason now their hand I'm holding.

My mind can't comprehend anything, all these people who were just simply living, how can this be happening?

I'm freaking from the inside out, I no longer hear the shouts, and in the midst of my body being submerged into the dirty thrashing water I couldn't part my eyes from theirs, who looked for refuge in mine.

As the selfish water consumed us whole, buried weightless in a mess of souls I do not know, but my compassion I wish I could show to my acquaintance who gave me one last comfort in the center of chaos; their voice and my voice really never were meant to cross, but our hands stayed together as our bodies were tossed, my eyes last resign was to the subway exit sign.

"We were just some goofy kids living and waiting for the tragic news when we got older, that life was simply waiting to fall down on our shoulders."

Keystone

I've never really wanted this before, but now the feeling is overpowering.

Isn't it something that something like this, such a sensation that flips your rotation, can appear out of nowhere like it's nothing?

This weird feeling that tears me into two pieces and releases two emotions I have no control of.

A part of me dances about with a smile grinning ear to ear the other is terrified, confined in a tremble of fear; this complicated feeling I don't want to label as so but another word for it I do not know, love.

Love is such a strong word; I don't wish to use it lightly.

Can this abrupt feeling one day develop into love; I suppose it is a possibility, but until that happens, this chambered emotion taunts me nightly.

Perhaps that's a bit dramatic, I know naturally I should be ecstatic, I just can't help the thought that you're too good to be true.

For if I let you in, let you take me for a spin, and you come to the conclusion that I'm not your resolution, I'm not sure what I would do.

There's a reason why my guard is up, why it's heavily guarded by unpleasant experiences, harsh lessons, and my own hard coated rationality.

It's there to protect me, but what really scares me is your unconscious ability to persuade me to let it all go as if you know how hard this all is for me, and that I've contemplated my definition of normality.

He isn't someone I expected to join me in winging this life rehearsal.

But when it's time for the curtains to rise I dare say I'd take his side; he wasn't what most might post as 'ideal' but ideally that's something I'd call special.

See look what you're doing to me already, I won't disagree this feeling feels nice, but I also won't forget my last attempts, I'm surprised from the past damage a part of the old me still remains.

I'm a mess you shouldn't meddle your hands in, for there's a possibility they could get stained.

My life feels like one big poorly planned parade for the underpaid, the clichéd, and but of course the hopeless writers of unheard serenades; now tell me how does that sound even remotely inviting or ordinary?

Your timing couldn't have been worse, but your presence couldn't be more necessary.

I want to fall deeply into whatever this is, because I kind of feel like I may need you more than ever.

But I'm afraid of endings, and I've never seen forever.

You are far more wonderful than any measures I can capture or compare.

I don't know how you do it; you somehow manage to delicately take my breath from me, even though I'm surrounded with air.

Your smile brings my mind to a state of home, you make me feel safe and not so alone, you become the highlights of my day.

The part of me that still lingers in dismay pulls me back the other way, for the inevitable is always able to catch up to my hopeful thoughts; this cannot last forever, someone will get hurt, and with that another piece of me that I may not be able to get back could fly away.

But that small fire inside me thinks differently.

Maybe it is worth the hurt to be loved unconditionally.

I feel absent in the world at the absence of your skin accidently or incidentally brushing against mine.

At the spark of contact one of us would apologize with our smiles, while the other returned the expression, and if I can make a bold confession though I didn't know it by your first impression I would without a question give you my time.

Time seems to move slowly when I think of you.

But in your company, it slips right through.

I may not have a firm grip on these affections.

I have a feeling you'll help me through the motions.

Though I may not be sure of what I exactly want, I don't want some pity plea.

I'm not perfect, he's not perfect, we aren't perfect; but that's kind of perfect to me.

In my fortress of comfortably familiar singleness, I'm not totally ready to leave my solitude throne.

But if we're taking bets on the life cards I will get, I will admit, you just might be my keystone.

Nesh

It wasn't a fairytale by any means.

At least not a traditional one, which was okay with me, I never felt in touch with the norm's love routine.

It was strange, but everyone thinks their first meeting with their love is strange; it's simply strange because we're never expecting to find love in such a place.

We met at a party I had no intention of going to, she didn't want to go but her friends wanted her to; I'll never forget the first glance of her face.

This newly bound hippie brought glow sticks to the party.

Some muscle headed guy wanted to try cracking them open and splatter it on people, he thought it was funny.

I had been there for maybe an hour and my drink was kind of sour; I was trying to navigate my way to the front door.

And as I almost reached it, a request to help connect a glow-in-the-dark bracelet rang over to my ears; something about this girl with her hair tossed up and a neon splatter on her cheek didn't want me to go anymore.

We exchanged names over the neon gaze; muscle man saw my face was bare of such colors and gave me a neon purple streak on my face with an intense high-five as well.

The moment I fixed her bracelet my life went from mediocre to swell.

I was afraid the next day she wouldn't remember me.

But from that strange meeting marked the beginning of our adventures together; a spontaneously neon we.

She was crazy and funny in a sarcastic way, but only once you got to know her well enough.

Her heart had been held and dropped quite a few times, so her armor around it was pretty tough.

I loved so many things about her though; she probably didn't even notice she did half of them, when I'm sad I like to think about those moments.

Like, no matter how last minute it is she always gives the best presents.

Or how no matter what time of year it was she was always cold; if it was socially acceptable, she'd have a blanket wrapped around her all the time, hot chocolate she'd never refuse.

Despite that all, whenever she got even the slightest chance, she loved to wear her bottomless shoes.

She begged me to push her in shopping carts when we went to the store.

We both loved to dance with white tube socks on, sliding along the hardwood floor.

She got the hiccups so easily, mostly from laughing.

Though when it first starts it's adorable and funny but after twenty minutes, for the both of us, it gets slightly annoying.

She took baths to escape; turned off the lights in the bathroom and illuminate it with a single candle sitting on the tub rim.

I'd check in on her, for she was usually in there for quite a while, majority of the time her eyes were closed; I was taken back that such a bright soul felt more comfortable in a world that was dim.

Gosh, even the way she walked, it was like the ground was forming under her feet.

She was someone I never thought I'd meet.

She was someone I didn't deserve; I don't know what happened to me.

Something inside me shifted, and soon the things I loved became irritating, the random dancing, her spontaneity.

If the light bulb was out, she insisted we change it together which consisted of me getting on my hands and knees so she could stand and reach the fixture.

It didn't hurt my back, and it was actually kind of fun, but when the task was done, I don't know why but I acted so coldly towards her.

I love all our blurry pictures; I wish we had more.

Sometimes I wish I wasn't the one who found her; I should have kept walking; I should have reached the door.

But now I'd do anything to hear that childlike wonder in her voice request a ride in the cart.

I never thought she'd be the ache in my heart.

Her escape wasn't enough.

All too late I realized I was guilty of holding her delicate heart too rough.

I'm told by other's it's not my fault.

Her penmanship says so, but I know; everyone sees her as designed in flaws when it's me who was designed with the default.

So now, I gaze at our blurry photos while wrapped in her old blankets.

It's hard to look at anything the same anymore, a life before her it's, well, it's hard to imagine it.

But when I'm sad, I like to think about those moments; I'm warned it's close to obsession, I try not to wonder too many questions.

It wasn't a fairytale by any means; it was a harsh one-sided lesson.

I took it all for granted, my neon girl.

I'm still taken back that someone who was always so cold could give off so much warmth; I'm so lost in this world.

I'm shaken, awakened, a hand touches me then.

Well, look at that, I fell asleep in the tub again.

Pier Boy

I used to live in a town that was quite small and known for its famous coffee and Great Lake.

My mother taught me her trade in cooking and told me I needed all the skill I could get for my sake.

Sure, I wasn't the best on the stove and didn't believe in what I was brought up to be.

'*A woman's place is in the kitchen and staying at home*', well that just wasn't for me.

While all the other girls my age were off sewing flowered dresses and waiting for bread to raise.

I would tuck my hair in my brother's cap and dress in his old clothes, a tad bigger than my size.

He would sneak me out the house so I could go do what I loved best.

I'd walk right into town with a pole in my hand, only worried about how well the lake was stocked, I could forget the rest.

Every time I snuck out it was the same routine; sit on the pier and fish and think about what my life was really meant.

Until a new face came onto the pier, that was the day everything became different.

He was a boy my age and saw right through me.

He knew I was really a girl, but didn't seem to care, he let me be.

One day we got to talking; small conversation we'd make.

Soon enough every time I saw him my eyes would sparkle, just like the waves in the lake.

Summers went by, and people changed their way.

He taught me not to be afraid; to go fishing as myself, and not care what the town's people say.

Day by day, hand in hand we would walk down to the pier.

And as we fished while the sun began to set, he would whisper in my ear.

"This old lake seems like something special now that I have you; my pride and my joy."

Smiling I set my pole down and whispered back "You've made everything special in this old town, my pier boy."

Little Ramshackle

The sky looked pathetic.

No, she didn't mean it; she just sees everything coated in a poetic aesthetic.

She hung up her coat and started to cry, she just wanted to be soaked up into the clouds in the sky.

Looks like the clothes still aren't ready to dry.

She sat against the washing machine as it rattled against her back, while her cries riddled off her throat.

The vibrations against her skin began to numb her, as if it was possible to lose anymore; her face she buried in her lap in the wrinkled fabric of her coat.

The fingers that hang onto everything but the things she truly needs tingled at the sound waves of her muffled cries.

She forgot why she tries; she can't forget the lies.

The room was black.

Her darkness had found its way back.

She had been running for so long, it must have found her when she ran out of breath and she had to stop.

Worry shook hands with anxiety that liked to spend time over analyzing and rhyming with her subconscious that was preoccupied with society; it's no wonder she could no longer hold back the heavy teardrops.

She felt cold even though she was wearing long sleeves.

She just desperately needs the darkness to leave.

Her knitted sweater held her together.

The warmth she was deprived of rushed along her skin that used to be loved, but she can't move sweater to sweater forever.

The washing machine timer is almost done.

Then it's onto the dryer and after that she'll try harder to rinse out the dirtier water within her; for now, she is able to wait until the clothes have spun.

Because the world isn't so sympathetic.

And perhaps the sky isn't so pathetic.

"Stay with me, I replied.

She was very kind.

She doesn't appear to have forgotten, but-

I have."

The Band Shell

She lit my world up like a sparkler in a child's eyes.

Her auburn hair danced in the air graced by fireflies.

The sun was just barley hiding over the horizon.

Smiling as though we're escaping the world, we live in.

And in a way we did break through reality.

For her gracious glow was the only thing I could see.

We quietly walked through the sleeping city to our spot.

Giggling and hushing ourselves so we weren't caught.

We reached our destination and ran up the few steps.

As she softly began to hum and wander in perplex.

I loved how carefree and peculiar she was.

I smiled but she stopped her humming and paused.

She laid down on her back and patted next to her.

Gently I laid down, a bit demure.

She giggled at my shyness and held my hand.

And for once, I liked this new feeling of unplanned.

As long as she was with me the world couldn't foretell.

Lost in our own reality of the band shell.

Invalid Number

Grandpa I don't know how many times I've reached for my phone to call you.

It hits me as my fingertips reach, that you won't be on the other end; the call will never go through.

But I try so hard to remember your voice; the strain has left me encumbered.
I can't even delete your number.

Grandpa I don't know how to get through each day but somehow, I am.

It hits me as I fall in bed, all the things you said; all the thoughts in my head get crammed.

But I try so hard to still imagine you here.

I see you sometimes, but you always disappear.

Grandpa I don't know who I am, or who you saw I could be.

It hits me, this weight I carry that I never let you see.

But you see me now; sometimes you're a face in the crowd or the streaks of sunshine through the clouds.

I can't help but wonder; do I make you proud?

My Intermission Girl

My life has always felt very busy, not so much messy because I can't do messy; I always kept myself working.

Whether it is little hobbies or tasks, or long-term projects, I lived for the feeling of keeping my pace fast, productive, and moving.

When I got to college, many if not almost everyone was surprised with me to see what my major would declare to be.

Though maybe it doesn't make sense to them because they see my potential somewhere else, theatre is what makes perfect sense to me.

For within this chaotic and at times ugly World there stands a piece, a pure piece, filled with direction, perfection, introspection, affections, that offers you nothing more than an outlet; a literal stage to create something new.

And how can I not be drawn to that; I want to build a World my audience can escape through.

My notebooks upon notebooks of ideas and handfuls of half written playwrights kept me pretty preoccupied.

As most of the day in small secretive writing spaces on campus I would be confined.

After some time of this I felt I needed to start taking a little break in the middle of my day, an intermission if you will.

I discovered I loved taking quiet strolls through the University's Art Program building; because if there are two things I love about art and its artists, it's the beauty that's poured into reality, and how they make life stand still.

So, this became my daily routine, walking the hallways and cleaning my mind of some of its clutter.

One day on my peaceful stroll I went past an open room, and from the view out of the corner of my eye I had to step back and take a second look at this painter.

Second is generous, my gaze lasted much longer.

A large open bay window was the source of the natural light that illuminated the room with a warm feeling, an easel stood next to it with its painter faced away from me on a stool; I don't believe, at least from what I've seen, I know her.

Every day since the discovery I had to see her progress, I had to walk past the room.

And every day she was always painting alone, her hair in a braid, but my was I never disappointed with how the painting began to bloom.

In ways I think we were similar, a bit.

She didn't like to paint, no, she loved it.

I'm convinced that she has been captivated by this love for so long she's probably grown immune to its fumes; she's got no lungs of an amateur.

I've come to the conclusion that her deep attachment to art is like the equivalent to my theatre; and holy man did I need to talk to her.

Because being in the presence of such a passion is an honor and before I could think my thinking over, I was already by the window.

Surprisingly I didn't startle her, or at least it didn't show.

With one more stroke of her brush she set it down as the room somehow got to a new level of hush, and she looked at me and my was I not ready.

For this whole time since this room's discovery, I thought I was looking at something amazing, but it turns out the art was faced away from me.

Her peaceful face was graced with a delicate grin.

Her arms and hands were decorated with clean captivating tattoos that set such a compliment to her skin.

"I always wanted to get a tattoo." I spoke, my anxiousness was clearly present, but she didn't seem to care.

With an inaudible laugh she responded, "You totally should, they're wonderful, but addicting, and it's crazy sometimes you forget they're there."

And there I was, I was suddenly stuck in my own profoundly fast paced life, struck by an artist who made me freeze in my own mind; all I could do was smile.

To my smile she politely laughed and told me if I'd like I could stick around for a while.

And so, she became my regular, but a spectacular spark to my ordinary days.

She would paint by the window, shine in the sun's glow, while I'd work on my writing and sometimes, at her request, I'd read her my plays.

One time I saw she had a brush with a very fine tip and some extra black paint on her pallet.

I felt giddy at the question that slipped off my lips; she most definitely probably thought I was silly, but as for the idea she loved it.

With her brush in hand, she motioned me to stand, as she then directed me to the bay window ledge where we both could sit.

I was worried this seating arrangement wouldn't work, but as we both hopped up sitting cross-legged across from each other, it seems I was wrong; it was comfy fit.

Our knees just barely touched as I extended my arm to her.

As she then proceeded to paint tattoos on me, at first it kind of tickled but after a few strokes I liked the feeling, isn't she something, something so pure.

She covered my arms and some fingers, with a collage of small, but detailed, lovely, painted tattoos.

There was a cute little camera by my elbow, along the left side of my forearm leading to my wrist was a crisp violin bow; there's so many I'm so amused, but I think my favorite is the little kazoo.

And in her eyes, I found something I could never translate into words or try to direct on a stage.

She didn't have life all figured out, instead she didn't worry what it was about; I dare say, I think she has become the introduction on my life's second act on the first page.

She has painted color into my life's backdrop.

My world around me has unconsciously become slower; now I can see the beauty I use to let pass me; she has helped me stop.

Maybe I can be her favorite color of paint, and she my stage cues.

She's my intermission girl, and I her lad with washable tattoos.

Senescent

'Welcome home honey, how was your day?'

"Oh you know, nothing new nothing old, it was okay."

'You're so silly with your sayings, I don't know how you just think of them, but you have quite a few.'

"It's just something to do, but any who, how are you?"

'Oh, don't worry about me, I didn't really do anything today, but I did see you still have to return that one pan we borrowed from Joan.'

"Well, I worry about you; you could have at least answered your phone."

'Honey, you know it's not working anymore, and I don't really like when you're alone.'

"Then we need to get you a new phone."

'Please not this again, honey.'

"What is this about is it about the money?"

'No, it's just, I can't do this.'

"Is there something I missed?"

'You're going to forget me you know, it's not even worth the chat.'

"My Dear, come here, why would you say that?"

'This isn't me.'

"I, I don't see?"

'You can't remember my voice, this is your own voice speaking, honey please try to remember me, but I'm not here.'

"I don't understand, I need your hands, Dear?"

Finding Jubilation

This rock could solve all my problems.

That's probably the stupidest thought you ever thought of, we've definitely hit rock bottom.

Get it, *rock*, bottom.

Okay yes, I have a problem.

I often talk to myself; I refer to we.

And I often find myself back at this rugged beach, and this is something they don't teach; sometimes you have to learn to be comfortable with being lonely.

So here I am with a rock in my hand, one half screaming in my head, the other wants to go to bed, and I have the weight of the world I'm trying to compress into this smooth flat rock.

My life feels like it's been on lock or am I the one who has the sunshine blocked; though sometimes I like to talk, myself I often mock.

But I'm not always rude to myself.

At times I stock some hope and motivation on my mind's shelf.

I should just go for a really long walk.

I just can't let go of this rock.

What's even wrong with me?

Is it something everyone can see?

Who am I trying to be?

Why does happiness come with such a heavy price tag when it's supposed to be free?

Maybe I've been chasing the wrong kind of happy.

Perhaps this weight on my back doesn't need to be so heavy.

I'll start by trying to let go of things I can't control.

And fill up the hole in my soul with laughter and goals.

Maybe I'll start playing hacky sack again.

Heck, I'm going to work really hard and earn a promotion.

This will all take some time, but this time I'm not giving into giving up.

I'm not paying attention to those who mention to look at the glass half empty or full, screw the cup.

Maybe I'm making it up as I go along but I'm taking up my own perspective for now on.

Because only I can see what I truly want, and I'll be riding this view until I've won.

I may have to visit this neglected beach every now and then.

But I promise you this; we will not feel like this again.

I guess my thought wasn't so stupid after all, I'm gonna miss this little rock.

I will fly with this wind; my fear and insecurity will no longer be my breeze block.

My feet are touching the shore's line, this rock is no longer mine; I loosen my grip and give it a good whip.

And with its release I swear I feel free and from this day on I'm going to be me; hey look at that I got four skips.

Haze from the Cello

The theatre was filled with well-dressed people, all being hushed at once.

For as I took my seat, my hands clasped on its arm rests, crossing my feet; anxiously awaiting the performance.

Nothing could take me away once the music starts, I had been waiting for this now going on months, if everyone could please hurry turning off their phones.

As soon as the Orchestra players take the stage my mind will be in a different age; it'll be as if I am entirely alone.

The chairs we all were looking upon were in a half circle, with a single chair placed in the middle centered.

One musician at a time came in, the audience in anticipation for the music to begin; when lastly the center seat, cello player entered.

My heartbeat had been steady.

Until their footsteps echoed upon the stage and into my mind, I wasn't ready.

Sitting down, immediately their bow ran across the cello's strings.

They hadn't even looked at the crowd, the Orchestra's sound so gracious and loud; but the music wasn't amongst the mess that has been created in my thoughts; all these floating things.

I can't see their eyes from up here, I wonder if they're similar to ones I've seen before.

They can't see mine either though, I could leave the show, and they wouldn't see me walk out the door.

How could I ever manage to grab their attention?

I'd be lucky enough to even find them after the show and steal a conversation.

Oh I'm getting silly now, my mind has made its own turn of desperate measures.

Thinking up a plan to be even just a moment together, perhaps I could than keep it forever.

But their solo chimed in, freezing those thoughts.

I'd mention a few, but I've seemed to forgot.

Imaging new things, beautiful but odd.

They weren't even shattered as the audience began to applaud.

Like how, if I could live inside a cello, their cello, I would hide in there for days.

Perhaps while lying in their baritone haze, I'll find myself dazed, and maybe it's a phase, but how can I not be amazed by the musical strings praising ways.

Goodness it's dark in here.

No, not in here, out there; my eyes had been closed, everyone had left and disappeared.

Consolatory Waves

I am terribly sad, and in a terrible way.

It wasn't even particularly a terrible day.

I've become overwhelmed, well it's been there for a while.

Impressive it is that though it's hard to even breathe I can still pull off a smile.

I miss who I was when I was young, but then again I didn't even know who I was in the first place.

All I've ever come to know since I fell into this darkness is this tear coated face, eyes soaked in disgrace.

I never said I deserved this.

It's dismissed; for how can I miss something such as happiness?

Something I haven't held, something that hasn't dared to touch me.

How could I be angry, can I blame something so beautiful to not seek out into such a violently dark sea?

I am rocked to sleep by the waves that hush to me my flaws that I've always known.

Truly then, I suppose, I am not alone.

Not alone, but not in good company.

For it's the demons in the waves of my thoughts, this ill-clotted plot, and me.

The Coffee Lady

Her smile was sweeter than any sweetener you could ever request in your drink.

And she would probably gladly step in front of a moving bus before she'd pour coffee down the sink.

She could always guess what flavor would suite you best for your day.

And she's never guessed wrong, I've heard people say.

Even if she was wrong you wouldn't say it so, how could you confront a heart like that, you'd learn to enjoy your coffee on the go.

So maybe she wasn't always right, but no one would ever know.

I always wondered what her nights must be like, when the hum of the espresso machine is hushed.

When the buzzing and snippets of conversations are long gone with the rush.

What does she do when there's no one there to smile to?

Does she remain the same for herself, or has the task become too hard to do?

I only ask because as I look at her now, I see happiness, but I also see someone who is very tired.

Aside from the dozens of mugs, day to day strangers that eventually turn into hugs; is there something she hides that she deeply truly desired?

Can she be more than the smile that wakes you up in the morning, serving up your drink that makes you function again?

Better yet, maybe she's set; perhaps she doesn't want to be more than the orders that flow from her pen.

I suppose I'll never know unless I ask her so.

But breaking the barrier of contently friendly familiar strangers isn't my forte, I can barely say hello.

The warm cup she's made me reaches my hands as her smile awakens the muscles in my face, she knows her coffee, that's all I've got to say.

Exiting the store, taking one more glance back through the door, I hope she's okay.

Flying Weather

Momma told me for a young little boy I sure had an old soul.

I really didn't know what she meant, but she's the wisest person I've ever met; she makes me feel whole.

Dad is a hardworking man; he doesn't say much but when he does, he's usually yelling stuff, I just do what I'm told and maybe he'll tousle my hair.

Maybe Momma meant I was different, because my brothers and sisters don't really play with me; sometimes I believe they hardly notice that I'm there.

We've been packing and traveling, trying to find a place to call our own.

And one day Mom and Dad found it; a piece of land with friends to work on, a house with a great big lawn, and a big silo we weren't allowed to play on; this is our new home.

As we drove down the dirt path that silently became my new racetrack, I looked out the window and saw a girl around my age playing in her yard, and I think she was staring.

I wasn't really sure how I felt when we got to this place, but life just got a whole lot more interesting.

That night when I went to sleep, I made a plan to run over there tomorrow and maybe make a friend.

Coming up to see she was sitting in the perfect climbing tree, she wanted me to come up, but a different plan I had in mind; we had a brand-new moment to attend.

We ran down the dirt road as I felt the grains of sand that kicked up from my fast feet hit my back, and as I looked just a little back, she smiled to me happily.

As I smiled back, she ran past me, and the race was on, we were on an imagination ignition spree; I'm just happy she sees me.

We reached our place where I wanted us to play, I told her we had to approach it quietly, I held her hand as we ran inside it.

The old silo, where we weren't supposed to go, but it was such a perfect fit.

There's a set of stairs that spiral around to the very top of the silo; there's a place up there where we could sit, and I thought from way up there it would be really cool.

Excited, as I began to sprint up there, she yelled to me, turning my head to see her looking to me like I was a fool.

I gave her a little laugh and reassured her to come with because there was something she had to see.

Mom says life is full of moments and I wanted this moment with her and me.

When we both got up there, she released her cares, she didn't seem so scared.

Sitting down and looking at our feet dangle, her hair was kind of tangled, but I liked it; the few stories up, down we stared.

We started talking and thinking, I was partially daydreaming; during our flowing thoughts, I thought about how no one really stops to talk to me, but here now I have someone.

A friend who likes to run, who seems to like to be in the sun, I believe an awesome friendship has begun.

I daydream a lot, Dad doesn't like it, but Mom says my dreams will come true.

I just have to believe, work hard, and follow through.

While I was thinking I looked to see she wasn't smiling.

I could tell she wanted to say something.

So, to help her along I started to tell her stories of all the places I've lived and how I'm glad I ended up here.

She softly told me how she's never left the farm, she wants to see new things, and she gets awfully lonely; I really wanted her smile to reappear.

Looking up to the crack in the roof where I could see the sky, I told her I could fly, the pause between us felt like awhile.

But then she laughed, and I laughed with her, I got her to smile.

Of course, she didn't believe me, and of course I couldn't show her right away.

I have to believe and work up to that, but I got her to smile, I told her I would show her someday.

Every day I would run super-fast to her house to build up my strength and then we'd go play pretend.

Through the rainforest of the sun flowers, our kingdom within the rock piles by Dad's field with the cornstalk towers; one day she told me I was her only friend.

I never wanted her to be sad.

And I don't think she could ever get mad.

Whenever she seemed sad though, or when for the day I had to say goodbye.

I reminded her of her smile, and that I'd show her I could fly.

I never felt like I had a whole lot of responsibility but now to me it was to make her happy.

Because we had our own little world and I never wanted it to end, she's my best friend; she's important to me.

Every day I would think and believe my very hardest, I could see myself flying, and when I get it right and I show her, her smile will last forever; someday she'll see.

It's okay that it's going to take a while because we get to play every day anyway, and I think it's funny when she says she doesn't believe me.

Then one hot day as we sat under her tree, drinking pink lemonade, in my mind I smiled at all the memories we made; and to this it was official, today is the day.

I was going to practice first then if all goes well, I'll show her, and if not, I'll practice some more; but everything will be okay.

In the perfect moment I told her today was flying weather.

With a roll of her eyes, she sighed as we laughed together.

Her Mom was calling her to come inside and my smile I couldn't hide as I waved goodbye and called out that I would show her.

I ran down our dirt racetrack as again I felt the grains of sand on my back; I ran with everything I had and the wind weaving past me confirmed today indeed was flying weather.

After arriving to the house and doing some chores I snuck out the door, everyone was busy.

I was doing this all for her, but up until now it didn't occur that if I could show this to my family, maybe then they'd see me.

Entering the old echoing silo, I thought what better place to practice then the first place we played; the sun was shining through the crack of the roof as I made my way up the stairs.

With each step I heard my Mother's voice in my head: believe, work hard, and follow through; I was prepared.

At the very top, the highest I've ever been, I didn't feel scared.

I felt content.

This is just another moment.

I clenched my fists a little, then released the anxiousness; I felt a smile come across my face as I closed my eyes and thought of her.

I could feel the pulse rush through my feet as I stepped forward, this is exactly what life ordered; to make her smile forever.

Warm Habits

Gosh is he something to adore.

I couldn't ask for much more.

Though I miss my sister dearly.

She doesn't really seem to miss me.

He always reassures me that everything will be okay.

We both loved to lie in bed all day.

Running my fingers through his hair while he softly hummed a song.

Once I got the tune I'd hum right along.

This warm, soft, comfy place made us feel so safe, casted away from the confusion the world left behind.

He knows, though, that my sister never leaves my mind.

He knows I have a bad habit of waiting for things that aren't going to happen.

He says he'll try but things may not be how they were again.

We helped each other get our minds off of all the negativity.

Like drawing pen tattoos on our arms, or taking turns reading poetry.

I didn't care what time of day it was anymore, it didn't even really cross my mind, until I heard a knock on my bedroom door.

We both looked to the small shadow casted from the light on the other side to the floor.

To my amazement I see it's my sister I thought didn't miss me.

I was so happy, but she was sighing, what is it that she sees?

She told me she was worried that I rarely get out anymore.

But all I need is right here, what would I do that for?

I don't understand her worry I don't like this tone.

She sat next to me; her hand caressed my cheek gently as she said, "You're always lying in bed alone."

Misfortunes of the Accordion Man

The accordion man sits off to the side.

To the side of the world watching its moments confide.

His music lingers in the ears of people walking by.

They don't see the accordion man; seeming the notes descended from the sky.

He has gotten used to this treatment though.

Closing his eyes while his fingers flow, continuing the show.

Each note that's released came from his soul.

Looking at his warn attire you'd never know, as he stands under the light pole.

You wouldn't have known he used to live a marvelous life.

Wouldn't have even dared to think he beheld a miraculous family and wife.

But that's just the outcome of a glistening, dreamful plan.

Now this is the life of the accordion man.

A Peek into Tom's World

There was a guy in my school who always acted so carefree.

Like nothing in the world could touch him, anything considered ugly in this world he didn't see.

His name was Tom, and he always had his headphones on, as he danced through the halls.

The music department was his home, lost in his own world, in which he saw no flaws.

Friends of his tell me I'd never find a character quite like him.

I'd love to hold a conversation, but I don't know where I would begin.

You would never find him without a smile on his face or competing for first place.

His world he created around him was different then the reality we all had to face.

Lyrics and harmonies made sense, rather than Math problems and Chemistry.

Everything he spoke had so much thought and passion; and I wondered if he ever noticed me.

After days of building up possibilities and scenarios in my head of how we would begin to talk,

Suddenly he looked up from the ground and ran into me, both of us falling in shock.

Quickly he reached out to help me back on my feet and apologized.

His headphones still in his ears, as he smiled and looked into my eyes.

Tom was a silly guy at times, which most allowed.

In a fake accent he spoke "The pleasure is all mine" and took a bow.

We walked beside one another, and said he was going to walk me to my class.

The opportunity to talk was there, I couldn't let it pass.

I smiled and asked him what he was listening to.

Taking a headphone out and putting it in my ear, I finally got a glimpse of the world Tom saw through.

He smiled as we arrived at my class and he said "I never caught your name."

I told him he'd have to meet me at the end of class to find that out, unconsciously starting a little game.

He said he had one more thing to say before under these conditions he'd agree.

He took my hand and smiled; "Don't go changing on me."

Missing

My Mother held me close, my Father kissed my head.

This would be the last time they tucked me into bed.

Of course, in that moment I didn't know, and I was too young to understand.

I dearly miss the feeling of my parent's hands.

For that night in my bed as I closed my eyes waiting for my dreams,

I slipped right through my blankets, my sheets, my mattress, right through each and every seam.

I don't know why I was picked, or who even made the call.

All I can remember from that night beyond that point was it didn't hurt to fall.

No memory of the time between my departure of my old life and the one I was brought to existed, in an instant I was just simply there.

Though this may be hard to comprehend looking down at my feet, myself, my hands I had no age no, well no nothing, was I nothing; it's like I wasn't completely human anymore, maybe I didn't even need air.

Cold, I'm cold.

I feel neither young nor old.

I had fallen into a single room, at first it was empty.

From wall to wall it was covered with shelves, for now they were bare, but in time an item appeared out of nowhere; now there are plenty.

It's the same item, but with different details, not one was the same.

Over my time here I have seen them appear; snow globes, each captured inside is one moment in time, and for whatever reason they are sent here, my new life in a still frame. I'm no keeper of time; apparently, I suppose I am the watcher of certain memories. I've tried to tie the moments together to see how they link, but as much as I think, there isn't a connection between them; these moments have never seen each other, they have just become my amenities.

After more snow globes came in, I learned what I truly was the keeper of.

Each moment needed tending to, I had to hold each one for a little while, to give it attention and not let it slip away or the glass will begin to turn grey, and the memory will dissolve; I try to keep up, but there's so many snow globes it's hard to keep track, I cry when I lose a memory, especially the ones that have to do with love.

At times I feel overwhelmed trying to balance my time between them all, but I remember when I had the fall and there was nothing in here; I am thankful now there's at least something and I'm not in the dark.

It takes a while for me to forgive myself though when I lose a precious priceless memory of two people who love each other deeply, then the grey begins to consume the delicate flickering spark.

I do get lonely.

Pretty often I must admit, and I can't help but ponder how long it's been I know it has been quite a bit, I'm always thinking about my family.

Overtime, this abundance of time I'm sad to call mine, the details of my parent's faces have faded.

I held onto them for as long as I possibly could, sometimes I can still feel the feeling of their hands in mine, it makes me cry to think how long they have waited.

I don't have interactions with others, but there is one thing that curls my lips up for a moment or two.

A snow globe that somehow ended in the back row on the shelf, naturally at the state of boredom I rearranged them to entertain myself, there in the light beginning layers of dust was a couple, dancing and twirling each second through.

I don't know how I didn't notice them before.

But it's still here, they've been dancing for ages, it doesn't matter anymore.

Their smiles looked so fragile; this moment made me breathless.

I couldn't take my eyes away, each time their footing relapsed into the captured moment again some part of me felt okay; it's an odd feeling, I can't express.

Their steps mirrored each other, as well as the gaze in their eyes.

Whenever I get spare time between tending and mending the memories, I reach back to them, whoever they are or were in the world didn't pertain to the gratification in this deafeningly quiet place they unconsciously brought to me, a person they don't even know to a place they don't even realize exists; in both of our perspectives there's a list of whys for the order of things that it, itself, continuously defies.

Is my existence one of its own, am I entirely alone?

Could I also be held within a snow globe in someone else's unknown room, just waiting for the day my globe is forgotten and it slowly turns grey; or maybe in some infinity I'm their favorite one?

My racing thoughts never stop to rest, if I have a rare spare moment of silence ironically, it's too loud, my ears begin to ring.

And within this piercing, thunderous, white noise catastrophe invisibly consuming me a tear streams down my cheek, my throat is tight I can't remember the last time I thought to speak; staring into this void I can't avoid, for the first time in forever my Mother's face in my mind is clear, as she begins to sing.

The muscles in my face, I cannot feel them anymore, my heartbeat feels echoingly slow. She's so vivid in my mind, I don't want to blink in fear she'll disappear; I don't want her to go.

I desperately miss her.

I miss my father.

Sometimes I pretend this is all just the imagination of the shy little me I used to be dreaming a dream so beyond my own comprehension.

But these moments pass by; into new snow globes I must learn to hold, filling this empty voided dimension.

If I was present in the real world, where would I be?

What has become of my parent's, my family?

Has it been a day, have weeks gone by, could it be well past their lifetimes and I'm just here forever in a tangled loop of jumbled lost time, a wistful pantomime.

The forlorn optimism stays in the back of my mind, that at one point I'll open my eyes, or if I could just send them one last message: Mom, Dad, I'll see you at bedtime.

Redamancy

It alarms me when I feel the touch of someone else, perhaps that's just me.

I'm not use to such a thing, the split surprise to my pores it brings, the sensation we crave but cannot see.

Just a simple touch of the hand and I was gone.

Invisibly stitched together, from now until we felt forever, their heart on me was drawn.

The simplicity of our affection held a special connection; more than words could dare to describe.

But in little ways it tried its best to express in a way more known, small forehead kisses, hooked arms on walks, those kind of lovely vibes.

Oh, how we loved adventures as well, the more spontaneous the better.

But one of our favorite things together to do was float around in our canoe, it was always canoeing weather.

We'd strap the canoe to the top of the car, sometimes we'd travel far, just to feel the feeling of getting away.

I no longer felt out of touch, I've never felt love this much; I wouldn't have this life any other way.

People may not understand.

That all I need is to hold their hand.

It's okay if they don't get it.

Or they just won't admit it for a bit.

Because there's nothing they can say to take this feeling away, these moments I have that I'd never trade.

Like running through the boat dock at night with a single lamppost as our light, or simply floating along with the sailboats in the shade.

Everyday together has its own specialty.

But there's one in particular that always comes to me.

Of course, it was a time in our canoe, the long wooden beauty lead us calmly off course, and we were lead in a different direction.

We had never been this way on the bay, but for a new unexpected journey we had no objections.

The sights were beautiful, well while it lasted; it began to rain down quite hard.

Neither of us wanted to attempt to fight the waves, in fact it got a little scary, but I would gladly be their guard.

I remember an idea sparking in my head as the lightning lit up the sky; gently I got off the small wooden bench and on the canoe's floor.

As careful as can be, lying down on my back they came next to me, we held one another; in our minds we weren't on that bay anymore.

Some water splashed on us, we giggled at each other, how silly this must look.

How I wish I had a camera at the time, it would have been the best picture I ever took.

This was everything I wanted to be that I never thought I'd see.

Out of all the canoes of life they could have climbed into, still they chose me.

We didn't need to always be hanging on one another to know we loved each other.

I know nothing is perfect, but this may just be an exception of it, I hope we never feel forever.

Touch is no longer alarming if it's theirs, I suppose it's something I grew into.

I'll never get use to this, and I don't think I ever want to.

she was a portrait of love

He was her  artist

Letters to Sam

Dear Sam,

I bet you're wondering how I am.

Or maybe not, which wouldn't surprise me either.

It didn't seem like you even thought of me much when we were together.

I wish you could hear my thoughts; you know I'm bad at saying how I feel.

I felt, I thought we were happy, together; how can this be real?

Dear Sam, I'm through.

I'm done writing about you.

Everyday gets easier just like everyone told me.

Even now as I look upon our past, I can't believe the things I didn't see.

I thought they were butterflies you released in my stomach, but it wasn't, you left me tied in lies and knots.

You no longer deserve to hide in my words and slip into my thoughts.

Dear Sam, I met someone.

Someone who fills my lungs with laughter, who thinks of the before and the after, who helps me appreciate the warmth of the sun.

There are so many things they've helped me understand.

How I deserve better than you, or how your lies so deeply encrusted in my mind; for the weight of the world wasn't really meant for my hands.

For the first time in ages I'm writing my own pages, I can finally stand tall and feel like I belong; I feel so strong.

I'm not sure where things will go with me and my someone, but I recall you telling me I would never find somebody, and you couldn't be more wrong.

Dear Sam, I am happy.

Someone wants to marry me.

So there you have it, you were wrong once again.

I used to feel devastated you were out of my world, but I couldn't be happier that things will never be the way they were back then.

In the end you were just another, perhaps not easy but, necessary goodbye.

For now I have arms that long to hold me, a heart that loves me through everything and fits perfectly in mine; the wait is over, I no longer feel the overwhelming need to cry.

I'd wish you all the best, but alas it's not my fault you had it and let it go.

Alas I'm thankful you did, now I have real butterflies, time for me to walk down with my someone and make our lovely abiding ties; thanks for the show.

Broken Guitar Strings

I loved the feeling of the blasted music's bass pumping its rhythm in my chest.

Surrounded by people whom I just met, and dancing with strangers; but to me that was the best.

We would dance and laugh like we had known each other for years and such.

But they always remain strangers, we never keep in touch.

My life consists of traveling and always moving along; really all I do is roam.

A light blue Nissan, my music, a suite case, and my memories was all I've kept close to me, I didn't even have a phone.

Attachment I couldn't do, and commitment was out of the equation.

I suppose maybe you feel bad for me, but I once held passion.

My heart used to be filled with ballads of sheet music and my smile never faded away.

That is until the day he decided, with me, he wasn't going to stay.

Now there are ripped up time signatures and broken guitar strings where my heart used to be.

There is a glaze that coats heavily over my eyes, covering then pain you cannot see.

So when I found I couldn't settle for stability,

I packed the only few things that have done me right; the highway is like home to me.

Some nights I drive until I see the sunlight break through the sky.

Some nights I end up in an incorporated town known for its pie.

Most nights I can't stop thinking about you.

Most nights remind me that you've ruined finding something enduring and true.

I've been listening to too much Cold Play and I can never fall asleep.

I'm so tired of this exhaustion, but it's the life I have to keep.

I feel the vibrations of screams in my throat, and it hurts; my demons have turned into men.

I need to be reckless and adventurous because if I pause, I'll think of you again.

[White noise]

There's a live studio audience in my head doing nothing but waiting for the chance to laugh.

And agree to disagree but when the airtime is almost done, I doubt anyone will stick about for an autograph.

Loud silence often fills my empty spaces, its bittersweet tones are kindly cruel.

Knowing I'm clearly confused, but sometimes I'm a clever fool.

I need to start by stopping these racing thoughts that know no definition of a speed limit.

No one can see the controlled chaos in me; please press down on my start button and hold for just a minute.

Going nowhere is exhausting and I don't need a new routine; I don't mean to be straight forward, but this just isn't a quick fix.

There's a balanced insanity shaking in the calm winds within me; it's nothing much, just a numbing feeling to throw in the mix.

Oddly enough I've got a dim light inside of me, but I'm still an extremely average display.

My life is an educated guess, a calculated error; I made it past the multiple-choice section and now it's time for the written essay.

Yet I can't find a word to say, and yesterday can't set me free, my anxieties are old news to me.

Social outcast from the start who didn't want to be casted a part, but now floating towards the bottom I see this sea is lonely.

Easy problems I wish I had, that could make someone mad, because compared to others I've had it awfully good.

Lifting my head up every morning, dying to reach some part of life that will make me feel alive; I really can't be that misunderstood.

Fighting the feeling that I hate knowing I'm someone's least favorite.

And autopilot isn't an option in the calm storm, it's consistently inconsistent, and so I've completely destroyed it.

Goodness me, well I may not be a daily special, some days I may feel like a neglected TV channel, but I think I missed the big detail.

A dull light can grow its shine and it's kind of beautiful that it's mine; I'm a perfect screw up to learn from, and this studio is not for sale.

I'll throw a farewell reception to my mind's unreachable expectations; it may be a party for one but that just means more cake, time to learn to dream while being awake.

Never again will I let myself feel like a deliberate mistake.

I always wanted you to be
my Peter Pan,
and I wanted you to call
me Wendy

Frozen Forever

My footsteps are so light as I quietly walked to my bedroom door.

Quiet I must be, for I do not want to be seen, I wasn't like this before.

I used to proudly wear my metals of bravery, until the day of the terrifying rage.

The day we found many golden stars locked up in what seemed like hell in a cage; that day everything changed.

The beautiful children whose lives hadn't even begun always come to stroll through my mind.

They ask me why I hadn't come earlier to save them, why everyone is not kind.

I'd often cry and ask myself the same things as I cautiously open the door.

Climbing into my bed the sheets wrapped around my body, so tired and sore.

I keep my light on so I can find my way back from my dreams.

The sheets cold as a stream, as my eyes close, I drift away from the lights bright gleam.

I drifted off to the place that was the source of my rage.

I had fallen into the cage.

There was no sign of life, nor golden stars, but out a ways, a pile of shoes with no ties.

Getting up and walking down the gravel path, something flashed through the corner of my eye.

So quietly I stopped, so quietly I breathed.

I felt as if something was watching my every move, but it wasn't guaranteed.

Frightened with what could have been my imagination, or the presence of one of the men with no conscience.

I began to run so quickly without a glance.

I ran with all the strength this old body had left feeling my legs beginning to fall.

Collapsing onto the grass, without a person to call.

I woke up in an unfamiliar place.

A small cottage it appeared, as I looked, my possessions not a trace.

The room was gloomy; the walls were old wooden planks, decorated with old black and white pictures.

Looking closer into them, I felt my eyes get bigger.

They were the pictures of the children I came too late to save.

Stepping back as their eyes pierced into me, it's been so long since I've been brave.

I ran out the door to find myself in a small field filled with snow.

I thought it was just me and the cottage, a mistake I'd soon know.

Suddenly the sky turned back, and the ground started to shake.

Falling on my side then falling upside down to the sky with all the little snowflakes.

Free falling into what I thought was nothing; I hit my head and went crashing straight back to the ground.

I slowly lifted my throbbing head as the sky was clear again, the snowflakes falling down.

Looking out ahead while still holding my head.

I saw what looked like someone sleeping in my bed.

I tried to walk closer to it, but I walked into something hard, as I fell onto the snow filled grass.

Standing up, I discovered it was glass.

I stood right to the edge of it and saw I was in my room, placed on my dresser.

So confused and lost I tried to figure out what had occurred.

There was a sudden pounding on the door, I then realized it was me still sleeping in bed, as still as a display.

Bursting in came then men with no conscious, the reason why I stay so quiet, they're coming to take me away.

I pounded on the glass so hard trying to wake myself up.

My effort was useless; no sound of mine could be picked up.

One of the men covered my mouth as the other began to hit me.

Suddenly I couldn't see.

Faintly I could hear whispers as my vision started to fade back.

I was still in the glass sphere, turning around in my tracks.

Unknowingly I turned to a crowd of striped people so bruised and covered with scars.

Each person patched with a golden star.

My heart began to race as I looked down and saw the most fearful sight.

I was clothed with a golden star, and stripes of black and white.

My room was out of sight, I couldn't find my light, I was trapped inside my own world with no help, no help whatsoever.

Standing in the winds of the snowflakes, frozen forever.

My Heads-up Penny

This is us, and this is me.

Just a person who was living their life quietly.

Then you kart wheeled your way into my life and made it your signature messy.

It's a good kind of crazy, now that I have it, I don't know what I'd do without it daily; anyway, you taught me life isn't always tidy.

You couldn't express enough how often I should laugh and not worry about doing it quietly.

Well, obliviously take that appropriately.

You love to take my hands and dance with me slowly.

And I live for the moments where everything beyond you is blurry, my world is in no hurry, admiring your beauty; I love when you get all smiley.

In my dreams you have heads up pennies for eyes and your hair is always tangley.

You're always the first smile of my day, and I don't say that lightly.

Now I can't express enough thankfulness to you for turning my blue life into a yellow so vibrant and lively.

I'd be so lost without you, especially lately.

You have given me so much of your time; please may I ask you a question politely?

How does a most certainly happy, colorful, beyond wonderful eternity sound for you and me?

Crestfallenly Enshrined

Her name was Aesthetic, and she was beautifully lost.

You'd think at the sight of her, her smile would come at a cost.

But she shared it with everyone who needed one.

A smile for him, then one for her, until everyone around her was happy; but she never felt done.

Soon enough you could tell when her eyes looked empty.

There were so many things she wanted to be.

She wanted to be the girl with a flower placed in her hair.

But no one had ever put one there.

She wanted to smile without feeling pain.

To be like something, other than rain.

Because some people love rain despite that it's sad.

To look in the mirror and see a happy girl is a dream she's always had.

Dreams and wishes all curled into an image of a safe, peaceful place.

Somewhere she goes, that only she knows; a tiny refuge in her mind with a little bit of light left that she could embrace.

She dreamt of the beautiful life beneath a wishing well.

Where she could be free and see all sorts of wishes unravel.

But she knows dreams from reality.

These are the eyes she will always look through, but in her reflection never truly see.

She still gave everyone her smile.

Still discreetly visited her wishing well every once in a while.

Above all her wishes, there was something she was waiting for.

A life where she no longer needed wishes anymore.

You'd think at the sight of her, she had it all together, all her boxes were crossed.

When in reality, maybe, Aesthetic is perpetually lost.

Love across the Street

I saw her amongst the crowd, among the busy people.

I knew she hadn't even noticed my presence, but that kept the moment all the special.

She was on the opposite side of the street from me, beginning to turn the corner.

I had a list of things I had to do, but my eyes could not look past her.

Without a hesitation in my nerves, I booked it across the street.

It hadn't come to mind I was sprinting in traffic, but this beauty I had to meet.

She walked with the many people, all traveling to different places.

I only saw a glimpse of the front of her, and still I knew she was so much more then these passing faces. I gently pushed my way through the people, not taking the rude remarks to heart.

Her long chocolate brown hair laid down on her shoulders and met halfway down her arm; we were only moments apart.

I reached my hand, placing it gently on her shoulder as she cautiously turned around.

Her expression of my presents eliminated the world's sound.

People rudely and angrily told us to move on and keep walking.

But as the smile came across her face it became contagious, and to think, we hadn't even started talking.

Still looking in her eyes I smiled and admired her every feature.

While searching through her crisp brown eyes I couldn't believe I was meeting her.

I had no idea I would see such a heavenly face when I looked across the street nor the smiles and adventure today would bring.

As she took my side and smiled, I had no idea we were falling in love, but that was the best thing.

"We say 'we' matter.

They give us pity,

They grew careless and took too much."

Breeze, Trees, and Company

Her aesthetic was midnight waffles on a newly opened Tuesday.

She was trapped by such a force her eyes saw as love, when in fact he was a crow, and she was a dove; she finally got away.

He was a dead-end sign she chose to ignore.

When it was all said and done, that's when she came to my door.

A plan in her head, pain still lingering in the cracks of her heart, more than ready to leave.

With me in the passenger seat she wanted to drive across the country until we maybe found something better, perhaps it was naive but for right now it's all we've got to believe.

The essentials in the trunk, room for random tourist junk, mix tapes that overflowed the glove compartment; everything from sad-emotional to not-a-care-punk.

Maybe if one day we find this unmarked, self-seeking refuge this pain in her would have shrunk.

So here we go, no one in our little town knows; through the seasons and months we have to look forward to.

Not a prospect to our name, no rules to life's game; she chose the directions, I manned the radio, besides that we didn't have a clue.

We took a lot of pictures, met some interesting people, and heard quite a few stories.

Along the way we lost most of our worries.

She fell in love again, with the vibes of Carolina but felt more at peace in Montana.

I felt like the streets of Virginia knew my name, but I was really digging Minnesota.

The moments I fell for were in the passenger seat at night with it tipped all the way back, watching the city lights pass and dance on the car ceiling, I'll never forget.

I knew she was enjoying herself but until a few minutes ago I didn't think she had a favorite thing on our trip yet.

We found ourselves in the middle of nowhere in Wisconsin on a beaten deserted path at dawn.

Why are we driving so early, don't ask me, I'm surprised I haven't yawned.

With no idea where we are, she got out of the car with such determination and started walking.

Quickly I followed her; I don't think she heard me talking.

Tired and dazed eyed I followed behind.

Completely too tired to mind what on Earth we'd find.

We walked through the trees that held secrets we didn't know, and the morning breeze took them away.

Right now, nothing seemed to faze her, not even if these trees began to whisper; she was being pulled to something, I think, I couldn't say.

We climbed down a hill, through more trees, and tall grass.

I couldn't even guess how much time has passed.

Concentrated on my steps I didn't see she had abruptly stopped in her tracks.

Looking up, now the sounds I unconsciously blocked out were fading in; she turned her back.

She took a seat leaned up against a giant tree and motioned over to me.

Sitting next to her of course was a view but nothing quite like what we've stumbled upon to see.

Our backs against the bark, proud of our embark; the breeze didn't even make us shiver.

We were too captivated by our discovery of a somehow, calmly, overflowing river.

Her smile while gazing upon this wasn't wide but it was bright.

I couldn't part from the sight.

With the sound of the water finding its way and the picture now painted in our minds, she scooted back and laid down patting the spot on her right.

Politely I acceptingly took the invite, lying down as I look up to the tree's leaves that are holding on tight.

I'm not sure how long we laid in silence; my eyes had been shut as I listened to the water.

She cleared her throat; I opened my eyes, the water stirred.

She asked me if I missed my family.

My mind hoped they missed me.

"Of course", I softly responded.

All she did was nodded.

"It's a scary thought" she softly said, "to wonder if you're missed."

"Why?" I insist.

I heard her breath deeply.

She didn't face towards me.

"I thought I would be that girl who didn't care if someone was by her side, I don't even know who I am anymore."

"He stripped me of all the progress of who I thought I could be, at the time I didn't see all the lies he disfigured into promises he swore."

"You're wrong" I said.

She turned her head.

"You're right that he hurt you, I hate him too, but don't you dare give him that power."

"He didn't know you at all, sure he gave you the rain shower, but you're your own seed and now indeed it's your time to bloom into your own beautiful flower."

It was quiet for a few moments, the overflowing water's rhythm flowed black to my ears.

She didn't seem sad; I saw no sign of tears.

Actually, from the corner of my eye, I think her smile was slowly coming back.

As mine did the same, my eyes closed again to a comforting black.

Now the trees had their whispers, though she didn't say anything.

And the breeze twirled our way and sept them away, as she put her hand in mine, and I now had my new favorite thing.

The King

Imagine, their voice caressed as their arms pulled me to their embrace.

Imagine our future together, what seemed like forever; a dream I was willing to chase.

Imagine the adventures we'll take.

Imagine the promises we'll make.

Imagine our visions becoming true.

Imagine a life, with just me and you.

Imagine; this word that briefly held a larger meaning I could barely wrap my mind around.

Imagine the sound of a heart falling to the ground, shattered to be found the King I had crowned.

Imagine looking to someone who only a split second before was holding your world.

Imagine the hesitation locking in your body as you watch it slip from their hands, as they walk away from the unfurled.

Imagine the shattered pieces among your feet.

Imagine; I simply don't have to, for you're only riding my view from the backseat.

Imagine this now, now that you seem so intrigued.

Imagine reaching a chapter in a book that you couldn't come to read.

Imagine the book always open to that page, stuck in the chapters before.

Imagine, imagining meaning nothing anymore.

Imagine their voice while reading the words they once said.

Imagine the pain as you finally read ahead.

Imagine the tears that stain on their last words you can't dare to let go, your world is on pause.

Imagine, they said, imagining is all it ever was.

The Munificent Worthwhile

She liked to climb on top of the hay bales, a leg on each side.

With an arm extended down, scraping my feet on the hay as a few stray strands took to the wind to glide.

Out of reach of an outside sound.

Outside of our own universe that spun us around.

Because the sky seemed like ours, and the tall grass only danced for us.

The clouds stirred clear, as the golden sphere's rays held the blue painted sky together like a truss.

Endless rows of corn out in the distance, out of my eyes reach even from up here.

But that didn't matter after all, my eyes were enthralled; everything beyond us has disappeared.

The hills before us weaved into one another; the grass leading down to our bale couldn't have been more green.

In fact, it was the greenest green there had been that I'd seen.

The valley's deed engraved the pages of our souls; a letter faded within each memory seized in this spot.

If it wasn't for the sunshine in her that navigated our plot to peace we never would have thought; now she has me tied up in her knot.

Above our heads we overheard the delicate whistle of the birds.

Below our feet, kept the beat, of the swaying pasture, still after all this time in the valley that has passed, we hadn't said a word.

But what words could describe the way the sun tangled in her hair, and that matched the brightness of her smile?

Nothing could capture this scene; the munificent worthwhile.

Hiraeth

How are you today my Dear?

'I'm doing okay, you know it's been a rough year'.

But we have each other, don't we?

'Of course, always honey'.

I miss embracing you closely.

'Not as much as me.'

You always were stubborn, but I love that about you.

'I miss all the little things that you used to do.'

What do you mean- oh, I think someone is at the door?

'I'll get it, I wonder what it could be for?'

It's the kids, they've come for a visit, how nice of them to come out this far!

'I'll be right out, how about I just meet you at the car?'

They're leaving already, but they didn't even say hello to me?

'Honey I'm going to go have some dinner, just for a while, I have to leave'.

Can't I come with too?

'Please don't make me say it, don't make me say goodbye again, it hurts too much, I love you'.

The love of my life has disappeared but our conversation from before is now clear.

For I keep forgetting, I'm not really here.

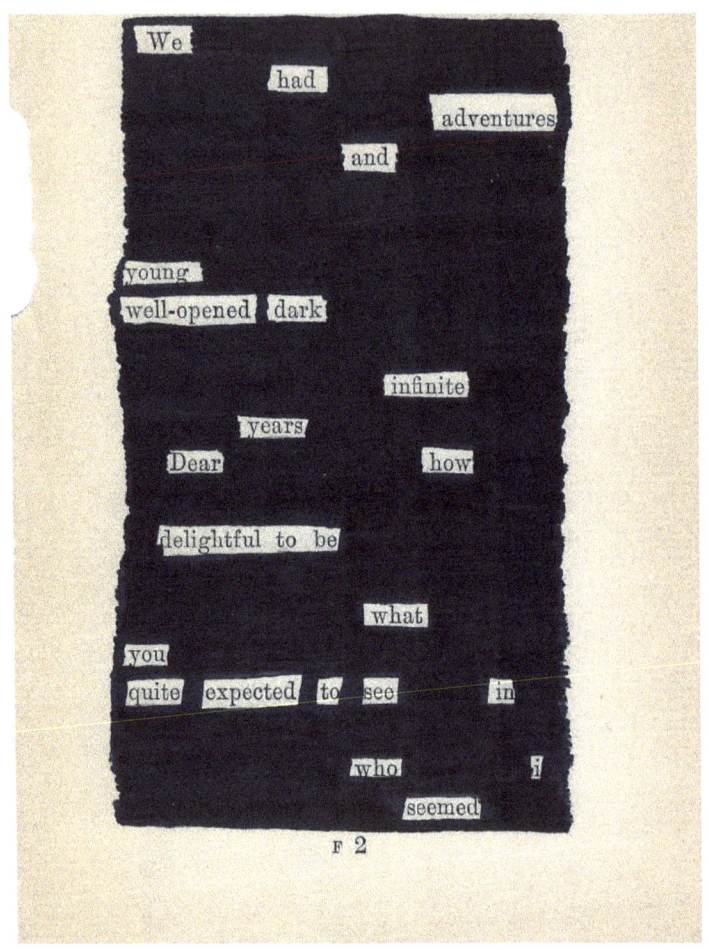

"We had adventures,

And young, well-opened, dark, infinite years.

Dear how delightful to be what you quite expected to see in who I seemed."

Detached

My mind is full of scattered thoughts but not thought up on my own.

Oh, how could I take credit for such things, how could I be alone?

You've tried to hide I see.

Yes, you have tried to hide from me.

I catch you now and then peeking around the corners you think I don't see.

Assuming I didn't notice when I saw you through the reflection of my coffee.

Aren't you so clever, slipping ideas into my head?

I never could figure out what makes you say the things you said.

But tonight, I've had enough; it's time for you to leave.

No, I don't want to hear your thoughts, this time I don't believe.

Do you believe I didn't realize what was going on?

Because walking past the mirror I saw that you were gone.

Why do you sneak away and come back with such haunting schemes?

Why is it I never fall deep enough to escape away into dreams?

I've always hated what you've created; you used to be apart from me,

I can't tell the difference; I don't know what else to be.

Sometimes you just don't know, and sometimes that's just okay.

Your visit is long overdue, soon people will see me like you they'll see right through, please don't stay.

Please leave the scattered pieces I'll fix it on my own.

Looking at me people would think me lonely but we both know I've never been alone.

And if the angels can hear me when I shout out into the air, hoping it will drift to someone that will listen and with that you'd disappear.

Let them know I wasn't always like this and I wasn't always here.

A Pirouette's Silhouette in the Technicolor Masquerade

Initially, this wasn't exactly the reality of the story I imagined I would be strolling through.

Madness intertwined in my balance; due to the absence of the clarity I sadly never knew.

Submerged within my story drips the coffee stains of a constant worry that I won't be able to carry my own words.

Tucked away amongst these fears harbored in a bay of tears is the masquerade I've made, as I sometimes waltz amidst my faults listening to my treasured records.

Impacted while surrounded by the melody that keeps me on my feet.

Listening to the lyrics composed by someone I've never seen in my appearance, yet my thoughts they have complete.

Layers upon papers; rhymes and feelings I never spoke.

Faraway in the clotted grey jotted thoughts, sometimes astray but it always finds its way, I remember I am broke.

Imagining I could erase and then replace the haunting flashbacks in my head.

Glossy eyes make for a foggy story; I hate to worry, so I throw it on paper instead.

Undoubtedly you see I am not clear on who I want to be.

Riddled in tattered sin, I've lost where to begin, it's a mystery to me.

Impolite to interrupt, I'm sorry it's abrupt, but I must ask.

Nevertheless, now politely I request, how often do you take off your mask?

Granted I confess of course I linger in my own stressful mess, trying to sway away the grey.

In case the news didn't get through, someday things will be okay and it's okay if it's not today.

The day I get up every morning to find, and always keep in mind when I'm accompanied by emptiness.

Optimist perhaps I am, but while I'm here, past the tears, still dancing in my masquerade I will keep searching for my happiness.

Unfortunately, this may not be the response you were hoping to receive, but fortunately I reveal I've left some signs.

Though hidden you will see if you look closely, I've left my answer in these lines.

Queen of Diamonds

She was brilliantly witty.

Oh, so pretty.

Even the unraveled fabric from the hole in her jeans looked like some form of art.

It seemed like there was always some kind of vision, a script, playing through her mind, I'm not sure if it was connected to her heart; I just hope I had a part.

She'll dance when she wants to, and when the music's through she'll leave you alone.

She'd never admit that she misses the feeling of home.

She wouldn't admit she was a rebel, course that's something a rebel would say.

I could try to understand her, but there's just no way.

You'd never truly recognize her disguise.

The only constant you'll see is the thing she can't help but be it's in her tired eyes.

I think she knew I was trying to figure her out.

One day she told me she was doing the same, I had no idea what about.

But it seemed she wanted me to stick around for a while.

I'd do close to anything to see that smile; I'd change my style, run a thousand miles, alright maybe not that but it's a pretty big pile.

She's just so lovely to me, even if it's something only I can see.

Even if she doesn't believe me.

She never failed to remind me that I was wasting my time.

Claiming I'm starring at a blank portrait, one that hasn't even been pained yet as a matter a fact, but I always argued she was doing the same with mine.

"Am I confusing to you yet?" She whispered.

'No, just a mystery.' I answered.

Why was she searching so much through me?

When it's not me who's the interesting one, I'm safe, plain, and boring.

There was a silence that began to frequently stir between me and her.

What words were running through her script, she hardly said a word these days her lips were zipped; inside her mind I've kindly tried to enter.

I'd hand her flowers; she'd give me the gaze of her empty eyes.

Blue skies she'd toss aside, sunny days were nothing more than a glare that annoyed her, and I loved surprising her with clothes, but I always bought the wrong size.

I was beginning to think perhaps she was broke.

But one day unexpectedly she finally spoke.

"I'm leaving" Her eyes stained my racing thoughts.

I couldn't move; her mouth is moving but I can't hear, how can this be happening after all the negative scenarios I've fought?

Her voice pierces in.

Take me back to our beginning.

She told me I was trying to find her, when really it was impossible, because there was no one there.

She had no clue who she was or wanted to be, but she figured out me apparently, and now she doesn't care.

Torn apart, she tore the layers off my heart.

It hits me deep to feel the shatter of the promises I can no longer keep; I never had a part.

I guess on the other side of the painted portrait you'll see what I truly am; I'm nothing more than what you want for sale.

I was the dried paint under her fingernails.

Denouement

I have found that recently my life doesn't seem to feel like my own.

Perhaps it's the feeling of the winter air caressing my bones I've never been able to outgrow, but in the tone of my reality, I feel alone.

I wear sunshine on my sleeve, but the night took up rent in my soul a long time ago.

It has gotten quite dark in here and I can't stand this feeling of being lost in my own mind, absent amongst color, a constant moving shadow.

This morning could have been better, along with this weather, if I'm late for work one more time I'll be fired.

I'm young I know, but I've recently acquired an overwhelming desire to retire; I guess I'm just tired.

The morning's population has its own vibe of habitation; by the afternoon the populations are mending together, it's a different world by the sunset.

This morning is still, there's a snowman on the corner who's missing a button on his invisible jacket.

The words I heard and said today I can't stop replaying.

After a while of arguing I couldn't even remember why I was yelling.

I think we'll be just fine; we can get through anything.

At least that's what I think of when I look at this ring.

I think in the reflection of his eyes I saw right through my own disguise; I finally saw what my mind blinded me to see.

What I was really becoming to be.

I saw a frightened little girl who was painted a completely different picture of the world and feelings highly unprepared.

All I ever wanted to do was find the right words to make her not feel so scared.

From an early age I suppressed a depression I didn't know was in need of a confession; I thought everyone gets sad and mine would leave upon my requests.

From an early age I learned life is a confusing process and nevertheless I profess at the loss of my compass I have been a mess.

As I drove under the bridge, in the review mirror I saw a kid run across.

All I can hope is they're okay; it's too cold to be lost.

I hope their Mother finds them and holds them tight.

I hope despite our fight me and him will be alright, since my change of appetite and my clothes not fitting right things have been a delight but a little uptight; maybe we'll feel a kick tonight.

At times I don't think I can handle this, and the future obstacles life will bring.

At times I have that overwhelming urge caught in my throat to run to my Mom and tell her everything.

The hands of my internal clock weighs on me and no one can see.

I just want to feel a piece of humanity touch me.

I wanted to feel like someone's miracle then maybe I wouldn't seem so miserable.

But I believe it's critical to have the right ingredients for a recipe of such significance; to think I'm vital is the first sign of denial.

How he hasn't left me, yet I do not know.

Why, I wish I could have left myself long ago.

He tells me I am a good person and I'm nothing less than kind.

But how good can I be if all there appears to be are bad thoughts in my mind?

As careless as the bitter wind outside the thoughts inside make me freeze in its selfish hold.

They whisper the things I fear, they make it clear, no one would notice if I wasn't here; I'm not crying I'm just sniffling, I have a cold.

I've tried to find ways to drown them out.

Their echoes always find their way about.

The louder my music is the less I can hear their noise in my head.

They scream *'can you hear me now'* and I don't know how to answer them; it's harder to ignore them when I'm in bed.

And it's hard to not sound crazy in your own thoughts as you speak out loud of these horrid voices hoarding in your mind to someone who can't hear them at all.

Describing them isn't an easy task and I am getting bad at wearing this mask; and so, they win again, I didn't think it was possible to feel even more small.

I have tried to do things to occupy myself so maybe then I wouldn't hear the dark and it wouldn't be able to get my attention.

Hobbies came and went, still the dark was sending in its rent, but one stuck with me and for a while released some tension.

I love to paint,

But life seemed to have its own set of complaints.

The colors that gave me life couldn't be my life sponsor.

Though each time I pick up a brush I feel an exciting rush, I know this much; though this I feel is what I was made to do that doesn't stop bills from becoming overdue, since then things have gotten darker.

He loved, he loves, my paintings and wishes I'd paint more.

I can't find the point in my mind; it doesn't come to me anymore when I watch the paint pour.

I've sat in the audience of the same empty canvas that mocks my eyes; I can see what I want to create but when my fingers meet the brush it's too late.

The images rush away from my grip, my eternally freezing fingertips; if the images make it out into the world the darkness will be evicted, and so they insisted to keep their stolen estate, and so again I shall continue this wait I hate.

Waiting for the day my eyes will feel wider and life will feel extraordinary once again.

And he will notice the pleasant change of my smile and hold me in his healing embrace for a while and ask me where I've been.

He is the good person; he is the good in the world I see.

Maybe I am a miracle to him, even after our stupid tossed words this morning he reminded me before I had to get going that he will never stop loving me.

Can't the dark see this, how can it want to tamper with such a thing?

I already can hardly see what use to fill so much happiness in me, how much more dark can it bring?

Though he can't see the chaos in my thoughts he believes me.

He refuses to leave; he will not flee; he reminds me I deserve to be free.

The dark doesn't care for caring things that make me feel like I'll be okay.

I try to remind myself every day that I just need to make it through the day.

The days pile up, they get heavy; in my mind I am sitting in a chair as the dark sits across from me.

Just the scared little girl in the company of all the things her parents warned her about, these bad thoughts attached and won't get out; maybe that's why she constantly says sorry.

The drive seems longer this morning, maybe it's the cold, but I will say I enjoy driving through the empty city.

To see the unoccupied sidewalks and unaccompanied shops, the streetlamps are still awake it's like taking a small break from within reality.

I need to replace this ratted jacket of mine; a lot of things are in need of replacing.

Maybe soon I won't have to go to work once I get farther along, but the farther along I get the more I find myself worrying.

What if I'm not cutout for this and one day I wake up completely numb?

What if the dark finds a way to leak inside of them?

I can't bear the thought of me being held down by the dark and witnessing it takes over.

Once dark marks its way it tends to stay and its welcome feels like forever.

I'm too afraid to open up about this; I'm scared it'll drive him away.

Even though I know he's going to stay.

My thoughts turn back to the chairs,

I wish my mind had a set of escape stairs.

I want to stand up to the darkness, to shout in its emptiness that I can and am more than its created mess.

I know I can and maybe someday I will, I hate feeling hopeless.

A few more blocks than it's time to clock in.

It's snowing pretty hard, I guess it could have been for a while, I've got too much on my mind so I'm not sure when.

At least there isn't much traffic, I hate driving in these conditions.

People can make poor decisions.

My windshield looks like my blank canvas at home; my wipers aren't much help as much as they try.

I need to just concentrate on driving, and like the wipers I am trying, when it's quite these thoughts just amplify.

A shock takes over it all with a slam of my breaks.

The kid that ran across the bridge has run into the street, and before our paths were to violently meet, I swerved; I've spun, I see snowflakes.

Maybe the kid is lost; now I've lost where exactly I am.

My head is throbbing, and I think I'm crying; my body hurts from the slam.

The hands of my clock and winding down, they scrape to escape my throat as I start coughing.

I look down to see I'm bleeding, and one of my buttons is missing.

I don't want this, this isn't fair.

But the world around me doesn't seem to care.

I want to tell him he's the last thing I'm thinking of besides to keep on breathing.

I can't stop thinking of his last words just as much as this body can't stop bleeding.

I didn't say the goodbye I wanted to, I don't want to leave; this has to be a nightmare.

Dark has finally let me go; my new company seems to be the ruined snow, as it drifts away, leaving two unattended chairs.

The story of me was

his closed door

For Me

I'm stronger than I thought I was, this strength inside me is what has carried me through.

Though departure has its toll, somehow, someday I will again feel whole; it started and ended with you.

Moments of ours hit me at times; I try to shake it off.

But it sticks around until its damage is done, like the start of a bad cough.

The cold winter air doesn't help.

And I suppose the old pictures will soon fade so new ones can develop.

You've made me laugh, but you've made me cry.

You have made me feel so small, no matter how hard I try.

But it's time I stand up to these waves that used to fill me with fear.

They may crash against me in attempt to knock me down, but to fall right now is not an option, my eyes will not shed tears.

For so long I thought my compass wouldn't show me which way to go if I didn't have you.

But the sun always comes out, no matter the amount of rain that comes through.

My shoulders have been tested with how much weight I can handle.

The pain my heart can take as well.

The future is all mine, and I feel so much open space.

There are moments I wish I could replace.

With everything I did, I did for you; I guess I was blind to see.

Your turn is over, it's no longer you; this is for me.

Mr. Meliorism & Miss. Celestial

She was utterly, internally, entangled by the moon.

It was adorable how excited she got when she spotted it in the late afternoon.

The moonlight tinted the frame around us as we walked together, sweater and sweater, in the mediocre weather.

Typically, on a night like this we'd stay inside and watch T.V. with blankets and tangled feet; but she suggested a walk where we could talk, and fresh air would be good for her.

My hand embracing hers as she was looking around with her half smile that I loved to make whole.

She walked a little closer and held my arm with her other hand as the wind began to pull.

It was pretty late at night.

Well technically almost morning, she held my arm tight.

The moon was still out but the sky was gaining its color back.

Some parts of the sky still looked black.

Along our stroll we came across a place we used to come together as kids, we'd race here right after the school bell;

The town's band shell.

I gave her a little grin and gestured to the memory.

She and I went up onto the empty stage where if I remember correctly, she first expressed she liked me.

We ran around the stage and danced for a little bit, not caring if anyone would see.

Just a breather from reality; an escape route for a journey, a new memory for her and me.

As I spun around to her, she gave me a weak smile I wasn't expecting to see.

Her voice was kind of cracking as she said she had been lying to me.

With confusion on my face and devastation on hers we sat down crossed legged across from one another.

She opened up her mouth as I was terrified what would come from her.

I didn't know if I should speak first or what I'd even say.

Before I did, she told me she had been lying when she said she was okay.

I saw the tears fall from her eyes so effortlessly.

I pulled her into my lap and held her closely.

She told me of her mind that used to be such a beautiful escape, like when we were young, had been falling apart.

The garden of her imagination, the trees of her will and passion, they were fleeting, and she felt like disappearing, and this was breaking my heart.

Her head buried in my shoulder, holding her closer as the wind grew colder.

I began to tell her;

"I will run through the forest of your mind and help you cut down your bad trees."

"We will plant new ones in its place and hang keys from their branches, a key for all your wonderful memories."

"We will walk through your garden together and gently gather your wilting flowers; we will create a brand-new soil."

"As we pat it down, I promise to never let you down, I will always be loyal."

"I'll dump my soul into this soil it is under my protection."

"You've told me that your life has no direction, my Dear, you are my definition of an exceptional perfection."

"We will plant flowers in your wounded soil, your life will be colorful; we will not stand for grey."

Her head lifted up as her glossy eyes looked into mine; and in this moment with her forehead pressed on mine, she was okay.

A soft and cold hand caressed my cheek, the other on my shoulder.

Our eyes were closed, and I was so happy to hold her.

Behind my closed eyes I could feel the sunrise, we didn't open our eyes; she whispered to me that she hoped that she wasn't being annoying.

With a gentle shake of my head that she giggled when she felt, and my hand graced along her face as I whispered back "I'm just happy I found you in the morning."

Until the End

"Will you stay here with me? I am afraid I'll die alone."

This is what he softly asked me as I made way for his bed, just getting off the phone.

I reassured him that I wasn't going anywhere; I was going to help him through.

An uncontrollable tear escaped his left eye as he smiled and whispered in a joking matter "Oh good, a party for two."

I'd known him for as long as I could look back, each memory stored in this old mind of mine had a snapshot with him in it.

We grew up on the same street, enlisted together and saw the defeat; it pained me to see so much life that once flowed in him was secede; now all he could do is sit.

"You remember when you saved my life?" He softly asked with a smile slowly masking his pain.

A forceful chuckle came out of me as I sniffled in response; "It's a good thing I saw that plane."

In silence, we reminisced the lives we both had, and how they repeatedly intertwined.

We were pals for life, and though he got me in a few scraps, his company was never less than kind.

"You remember when we met our girls at the party when we returned from the war?"

Once again, I smiled and nodded, remembering my only love from now to forevermore.

While I was lost in my own sorrow, he began to let out an easygoing sigh.

"Oh, I'm going to dance like I've never danced before in Heaven" he paused as I looked up to him, and he continued, "It's time for this soldier to say goodbye."

A spark of hope glazed over my eyes, as I wished he had just a few more years, a few more laughs with his best friend.

Grasping my hand, he spoke so crisply before closing his eyes "Soldiers, Pals, Brothers until the end."

No Vacancy

Someone had shattered them, you could tell.

Though I must say they covered it quite well.

You could hardly notice the small pieces missing; just little things, nothing to dwell.

Just things they used to enjoy but now seem to annoy, can't blame them though, how frustrating it must be to lose even just a tiny piece in a mess you didn't foretell.

Now there they go, checking into a mediocre hotel.

An attempt to escape a mediocre life in exchange for a room that has seen its fair share of strife; they were brought out of their thoughts from the sound of the elevator bell.

The doors open, they imagine, 'What if I fell?'

'Fell right down this shaft, with my luck tonight they would be understaffed, I wonder after the decomposing discover, how hard this old place would be to sell'.

Odd thoughts like these often come and go across their mind.

But anything to escape the dark ones is a-okay, they'd take the odd thoughts any day, their thoughts themselves were undefined.

They were undefined themselves though; they never knew who they were or even who they wanted to be.

Never bothered with a plan, because in the past they always fell apart; there really was nothing to see.

Nothing to see but this hotel room that looks like so many others in different places in different lives.

All trying their best to survive.

They sat on the edge of the bed across from a mirror not daring to look into it.

But they didn't want to just sit.

What was so bad about looking into it another odd thought, thought; what could occur?

As they look up, they began to remember.

It was dark, and full of words from the thoughts they didn't like to think about.

Once the eyes lock though, there's no coming out.

Forced, stuck to stare into this endless darkly thoughtful void full of things they deep down already knew but hated to see.

How love will not touch them, they can't even reciprocate the feeling on their own, they couldn't disagree.

They certainly are shattered; it's even more visible now.

When did this even happen, they didn't even know how.

But there's a lot of things they don't know, well would you look at that, they're stuck again.

Stuck in the black thickness of these thoughts; they, are my reflection.

my soul is kind of

achy today

I'm Here

She tells me she's done and that she can't do this anymore.

Her tears streamed down her face as she directed me to the door.

In awe I stayed by her side as her tears came out.

"Get away from me and leave me alone!" she began to shout.

She fell to her knees as I got down on mine, putting one arm around her.

Calmly she spoke that her life was just a mess; one big blur.

I rubbed her back and nodded as she vented on.

There were things I could have been doing, but this is where I belonged.

She looked up into my eyes as hers were still full of tears as she said, "I don't understand why you stay by me and why everything is so unclear".

I pulled her into my arms, as she laid her head on my chest; gently I whispered, "That's why I'm here".

The Lost Feeling of Love

Darling is my favorite word, for it reminds me of you.

Though I haven't heard it the same since from my world you uncontrollably withdrew.

You'd be so proud to see how much our boy grew.

Every time he smiles to me, I can't help but think of you.

He doesn't know yet he has your eyes and that crinkle in your nose you got when you giggled.

The steps I take getting out of bed each morning are getting less heavy; little by little.

The bed doesn't feel warm anymore though; I guess that's another thing I miss.

There's always an emptiness that consumes me from the absence of your kiss.

At times raising him on my own is more than I can handle.

Your voice still lingers in my thoughts, my Dear he is so fragile.

So fragile to the touch.

I always remind him you loved him so much.

I love him so much.

I love you nonesuch.

And though the softness of your voice keeps me calm when my vision is clouded from my tears.

I'm afraid one day it will disappear, but from a touch in my palm, things seem clearer as our boy appears.

His hand in mine, his smile it shines; how I wish he could see yours shine as well.

As he grows older, he'll see more of you in himself, won't that be swell?

But for now, as I try to cope with your side of the bed being empty, a burden so heavy; mixed in with the memories I can't get rid of.

Please remind me Darling, the lost feeling of love.

The Woodcarver

The woodcarver lives in a nice log home.

Where he carves, wishing instead he could roam.

He makes carvings of ducks, and maybe small bears.

Sharing his creations, and showing he cares.

The woodcarver lives alone, all by himself.

Putting his wooden animals on the shelf.

A woodcarver's life might be easy and all,

But his one wish was very small.

A life with friends, and family,

The woodcarver lies down; but this is reality.

Floating to the Sky

I walk along the board walk, so colorfully decorated in streamers and side tents.

Each tent had a new face, selling freshly baked goods or presents.

The ocean breeze floats along in the summer's heat; a high of seventy-five.

Smiling without a care, as the wind blows gently through my hair; so happy to be alive.

The couples walk on past, making way for the bench by the water's soft recurring waves.

They sit and exchange their thanks for being in each other's lives; a beautiful moment they'd save.

Someday I'd like to find love like that, I think to myself as I continue on my way.

Children's laughter travels through my ears, as young folks face their fears, this place is my getaway.

I may have come here alone, but I am not lonely.

For I know in time I will walk these paths with my special somebody.

I hand in my ticket and climb in the seat.

The ride begins to start up as I dangle my feet.

Out of everywhere in the world there's no better place where I can relax and heal.

As my seat comes to a halting stop, at the top of the fairs wheel.

I can only cherish a few moments in my special place.

But I do feel time freezes a bit up here, as my smile covers my face.

But life has an awful habit of turning our lives around into a funny shape.

That's why sometimes I close my eyes, so I can escape.

I think of all the moments when life didn't turn out the way I planned, and I wanted to give up and cry.

Tilting my head up and opening my eyes, right now there's no need for sighs, letting my troubles float to the sky.

"I suffer because a heart with sympathy loves upon the manner of pain.

I felt and could not give."

Soul Searching

Change and I were as good as strangers.

An occasional acquaintance I didn't quite appreciate its presence, I wasn't one for taking the chance on danger.

I like going to the same coffee house that's had the same artwork hanging up probably since the first brick was laid; I've probably memorized all the art's lines but still I find ways to get lost in them, to me it's not that hard.

Employees here have come and gone; new regulars have come along; every single visit I get asked it but I never follow through with getting a loyalty card.

One day I did the math, and it was sadly kind of funny.

Over the span of five years, if I would have gotten one, I would have had close to one hundred and eighty free cups of coffee easily.

I told her that once, her and I go way back, I can't remember when we first started talking it's hard to keep track.

She's the complete opposite of me, liberating, most likely subconsciously, free, she certainly doesn't try to be she always gets on me for not trying new things I don't get much slack.

But goodness was she crazy.

Probably not the type of crazy people would typically think of, but she was to me.

Its winter right now and she loves it, so there's one thing.

And then there was the canteen, yes, a canteen, of eggnog she would always bring.

She'd drag me out into the snow so we could go climb trees; I swear she knew how much I didn't like heights and plus it was freezing.

But her claim that it would be worth it to see the view was always true, even though the next few weeks we'd be sneezing.

'I want to find it' she exclaimed, slamming her hands on my bed right next to my pillow.

Of course, I, was, deeply asleep regretting the spare key I let her keep, and of course even though she has one I now feel the draft from the window.

I looked at my clock its 4am, what could she possibly need to find?

I swear I've been sleep deprived since the age of five; as I asked her trying to sound like I don't mind.

'No, it's not a want, it's a need it's a necessity.'

I gave her a strange look, which she did not exchange back to me; of course, this kind of thing is her normality.

"Alright, alright" I sat up wide awake now "What is this necessity we need to find?"

'I need to find it, my soul, it's out there I know, waiting for me to find it and fall in love with it, come on let's go I already feel behind!'

Now, I know she's crazy, but this was new territory.

Was she messing with me?

Alas this spontaneous lass was being anything less than serious as she started packing up some of my clothes.

I'd ask her what in the heck she even meant, but I know the routine on how this goes, you go with the flow.

When she wanted to do something, it was either now or never, rarely there's an in between.

I barely got out of bed when she tossed my backpack to me just by the grin on her face, I could see this was going to be one interesting scene.

We hopped in her car; the sunrise joined us for the ride.

I slept for a few more hours until she woke me up because I needed to be the map guide.

"You know, it's kind of silly to put me in charge when I don't know where we're going."

And to her response I didn't need to turn my head, I felt her glaring.

'It's important.'

'Just be patient.'

At this point in our friendship, I just shrugged my shoulders and said alright.

So, on we drove through the snow, the destination I still don't know, but of course still we took turns; she'd tell me to go left or right.

We stopped at little diners and munched on greasy food and deep questions.

Talked about our dream professions, reminisced our first impressions, discussed our own depressions, and made a few confessions.

She told me she cries more than she lets on.

I told her I often internalize my feelings more than I realize; I just try to lose them through a song.

And that brought us back to the car where we went back and forth showing each other different songs that brought a memory or a feeling.

I swore I was feeling something besides just worrying, this was more than something, I felt like I was living.

Smiling with some reggae music flowing in the car, she told me to get off at the next exit.

And of course, at her command we rolled up into a town with a hippie kind of spirit.

As she continued to give directions, I got the impression she knew this little place.

I got mixed signals if that was a good thing or a bad thing by the look on her face.

We stopped at a small art gallery next to the Swedish bakery and the water.

Walking inside to find some truly beautiful works, I followed her.

She weaved through the displays making her way to a big, framed picture.

She approached it like an old friend with a hint of hesitation, but it was like they knew each other.

The picture was of a little girl with a yellow sweater, on a tire swing, her back faced away from the camera looking out to the sparking lake.

I stood next to her; our shoulders brushed against each other's, I hope that wasn't a mistake.

A minute or so later we got back in the car; she drove us to a house another few minutes away.

A silence lingered among us, but that's okay, I don't think either of us really had anything to say.

She knocked once then walked in, following her lead I took off my shoes as she called out to see if anyone was here.

I looked around in my place and noticed this pleasant house has seen many passing years.

An older woman with white hair came down the stairs with a camera strap around her neck and the camera lightly moved with her each step; her smile looked as fragile as the vases by the door holding flowers.

They both hugged each other; I'm assuming this was her Grandmother, they were quite happy to see each other.

And my thoughts were correct, she introduced herself as Grandma, gave me a quick hug, and motioned for us to follow her into the kitchen and have a seat.

As we walked through the living room, she took off the camera and set it on top of the wooden half piano next to a framed picture, the same picture we just viewed at the gallery; I don't think my small gasp was discrete.

I heard a giggle from her Grandma as we sat at the kitchen table and I couldn't hold my curiosity in.

Politely I asked if that was her work of art, she smiled at her hands and confessed it was her husband's.

While she went to get the three of us some coffee, she began to tell me she has no eye for photography, but her husband was an excellent photographer.

She pointed to the back wall where I now saw it was covered with little framed pictures.

'You would rarely ever see Grandpa without his camera hanging from his neck, the world around him was an endless whim.'

I could see now he was sadly no longer here, and she would wear his camera around because she missed him.

They both went back and forth telling stories about him while we drank our coffee and laughed.

Our talks drew into the evening, more reminiscing, and looking through photographs.

Her Grandma gave me another hug before she went off to bed, and we exchanged our thanks of meeting each other.

Grabbing her camera on the way she walked up the stairs to her room, as the two of us washed the dishes from diner.

'This trip was for both of us you know' she said while drying the last plate.

I waited for her to elaborate.

'You learned to live a little more and not be so consumed with worry, and I made it here, where I need to be.'

She went on to explain that she was going to stay, and she was so happy to see a brand-new side of me.

I was sad at first, but I understood why this was her soul's destination.

Her Grandma needed somebody; this house is soaked with wonderful memories; this was the main place of her narration.

I hugged her goodbye, but she told me this wasn't goodbye.

We smiled to each other, and as I drove away, I saw her wipe her eye.

Back home now things aren't exactly the same but eventually something would have changed, but of course not my choice of coffee.

I still go to the same place and change still isn't exactly friends with me.

As I sit in this old place surrounded by familiar faces, I think of her often while writing to her on the back of a postcard.

"I finally got a loyalty card."

Coexist

I'm falling again, and this time it's bad I can feel it.

And I can't admit how much I want to quit; well I guess I just did a little bit.

It isn't funny.

I'm not trying to be.

I'm just really sad and I don't particularly know why.

Maybe at some point I did but that seems to escape me now and I'm too tired to try.

I lie every day.

How many times you say?

Depends how many people ask me how I'm doing.

But just assuming;

I kind of want to cry,

I kind of want to die,

But that is where I'm distorted with comfortable lies.

I convince myself and others I'm okay by hiding my cries.

The tears that dry onto my face, I'm surprised they come out at all; I'm surprised I haven't moved.

Am I really that surprised though, not that it's something I can really prove.

For the life of me… for the life of me?

That trade off seems kind of empty.

My mind is a mess I'm sure you can tell.

I haven't really been feeling well.

It's all this stress and anxiety man, I just can't shake it off, it's latching on.

It's a shame that education brings out my depression.

I've got too much circling my head.

Too much for me to lie down, if I do it'll weight on me and keep me in bed, so I say up instead.

I've been fighting to stay alive since nineteen ninety-five.

Sometimes it really hurts to strive, but I'll kick it for the drive.

Because there are people here, I need to vibe with, like life prescribed them to me to help me proceed.

Spending money I don't have on memories I need.

My needs and wants coexist.

My wants really aren't that big of a list.

I wanted to be the equivalent of the excitement that people get when they see their favorite color gumball spinning down the spiral tube and landing in their hands.

I wanted to be the special warmth found only in a person's favorite blanket while listening to their favorite band.

I wanted to be like the sunlight peeking through the curtains.

I wanted someone to love me and of that be certain.

But I am certain I am falling into this place.

And the curtains of my mind have blocked out the sunshine, but you could never tell by the look on my face.

I'm just another person insisting they're okay.

But I'm not the only one; they're just hard to see during the day.

Haven's River

Find me a river with those eyes of yours that wander free.

Free to every sight that fit your delight, when you swore before those eyes were meant for me.

Carve me a river with that big ego you behold.

Behold the cold waters, though untold, we both know you controlled.

Make me a river let me be your inspiration.

Inspiration from your temptation, we'd always been a rocky foundation.

Shape me a river with those large hands, clench your fists that never missed me, grind them into the Earth.

Earth, the sky, the stars up high; I thought you'd show me it all, I still think about it for what it's worth.

Gather up the river's waters with your words that always drew me in.

In the haven that I caved in, pretending you were a savior when I knew where you'd been.

Pour out the river for me; hear the wave's crash against the dirt walls you created.

Created unconsciously, now that's fine with me, this path was fated.

Find yourself another river for me; for I've waited patiently, our time is done.

Done and gone, time to move on; rewrite myself while sailing away on the river you had begun.

Just Her

I loved the way she sipped her coffee.

I miss the way she hated tea.

She adored vinyl records, but she didn't like having to get up to flip it around.

And even though she denied it, she loved the feeling of being upside down.

I loved when she would surprise me with hugs.

I miss when we used to eat dinner together out of mugs.

She used to say we were odd souls who weirdly belonged together.

And then she'd give me that smile that melted my heart; that was just her.

I loved to dance with her, though I was no good.

I miss how bad she was too, but that didn't stop us; of course, it didn't but it should.

She made me feel weightless in a life where my shoulders were always heavy.

And away the pain went she was heaven sent; it was like I knew her already.

I loved her.

I miss the life we had together.

She was my everything; more than anything I miss her essence the most.

And this has been me, stuck surviving between memories, talking with a ghost.

DATE	ISSUED TO
you	went behind
	society's back
and	society was ignorant
	and envious
it	took somebody
	your younger self

öde

I get up, I take a shower, I throw my jungle of hair in a bun, so people don't stare; this is my everyday morning.

A literal rinse and repeat as I brush my teeth and my foot subconsciously taps along to the beat of my morning playlist; I am the picture next to the definition of boring.

This particular morning, I wasn't aware that me and my wild untamable hair were about to be redefined.

Walking downstairs from my room to the living room my eyes locked in place to the thing misplaced; my mind took a moment to rewind.

Running back up the stairs dragging my roommate to the top step overlooking the living room I whispered and ordered for her to uncover what in the world she was doing.

To my surprise there was an easy flowing tone in her voice and a spark of joy in her eyes, I knew she was obviously up to something, but if her plan could be obvious that would be something.

There was a guy, whom I have never seen before, and a dog, which I really wanted to pet, sleeping peacefully on the couch with a blanket carefully placed on them.

The guy didn't look very old, the dog however seemed so as it laid in the guy's gentle hold; I asked my roommate where she found him.

And so, she led me to her room and began to tell me the story of the guy.

Taking place last night where she was walking to her car after work and a dog came running by.

The seemingly determined dog stopped in its tracks and turned its head to my roommate who was still looking at it and wondering where its owner was.

As she stood there wondering if she should call for it or let it be the dog came over, sat down, and lifted its paw.

She giggled and shook it like a proper greeting and after their polite introduction it softly bit her sleeve and ran.

She had no idea what to do, what was the game plan, after about a few minutes of running she found the dog brought her to a man.

The man did not see her; he seemed preoccupied just a smidge.

And panic began to settle in her voice, starring at the paths of fate in a stranger's choice, he was standing on the edge of a very tall bridge.

"Excuse me!" She cried out to the ears of a guy she knew nothing about, well other than his apparent unhappiness and that he may have a dog.

She described how the atmosphere played to his favor, no one ever really went here at this time of night, and there was a linger of a thick fog.

Startled the man held onto a pillar and pivoted to the voice, with a raise of his eyebrows he responded, "Can I help you?" with a hint of irritation in his voice.

"Funny, I was going to ask you the same thing." She replied, as she faintly recalled seeing the contemplation in the guy's eyes about his choice.

Eventually she talked him into coming down with a promise of a warm place to sleep for the night, but the real deal breaker was the offer of coffee.

His dog slept in her car while they had a cup or two in the Café of Blues; she told me how surprised she was of his tragic story.

He had lost his family years ago, explaining how he filtered in and out of the system until he turned eighteen and he had to go.

Sleeping in shelters when he could, one time he even made a fort in the woods, when she asked if he had any relatives it was a slow head-shaking no.

To try and make him smile she asked him how long he's had his dog for.

Her effort was shown as a smile crossed his face "Funny, I was going to ask you the same thing." As the words came out, she couldn't help but blush at his wittiness, as he explained he had never seen the dog before.

Astonishment covered hers, and my own, face.

"I guess the night had other plans for the three of us." He philosophically answered her unspoken questions; she left a tip on the table as they both left to go to our place.

Bringing me up to speed she told me when he wakes up, she's going to take him to a friend of hers by the dock who can give him a job.

As I turned her doorknob and returned to the top step looking down, I regretted my previous judgments of this guy, thinking he was just some homeless slob.

I took off work for the day and gave my roommate a hug that I think silently explained how I was proud of her for doing such a selfless thing.

Not that she's never did something kind for another person, she always did, but this was different; if she hadn't followed the dog and talked to the guy, I can't imagine the reality fate would bring.

Releasing our hug, the word kept imprinting in my mind; fate, what a strange thing.

How it silently stitches stories together, bringing sunshine to the unexpected mind who feels a constant gloomy weather; really fate can create pretty much anything.

So, this was my new definition; my roommate is a beautiful saint, our new roommate loves his new job and is simply great, as for the dog, she, likes to chew on my pens.

I'm pretty sure my roommates are going to fall in love, someday on their wedding day the dog and I will release the doves; you know, it's crazy what a wild-haired girl, a spontaneous heart of gold gal, an inspiring hope filled renewed guy, and an intelligently, pen eating addict dog have in common.

Promise

Why, this is a surprise,

How blessed are my eyes,

That you are holding me;

It's me you choose to see.

You are just delightful,

And I am grateful.

The way you hold my page,

You break me of my cage.

Has anyone ever told you,

You are the best queue?

Because it's true, you are,

You are my shining star.

Your fingers hold my words,

My heart has no guard;

Read my words forever,

Promise you'll remember.

I'm smiling look and see,

You did this to me.

Your smile is so lovely.

Please be happy with me.

You can be happy too.

Happy; me and you.

Your smile is my treasure,

I'll give you forever.

This paper holds me closed,

You make me exposed.

Please do not stop reading.

Remember me smiling?

You can't just leave me here,

I will disappear.

You promised to stay here,

This is what you want my Dear?

I didn't choose to be trapped within the fibers of this page; so welcome, welcome to the snapped writer of the backstage.

So what is a promise but an empty bliss, oh you want words I'll give you this; so you want to leave me, well I hope you're ready to be upstaged.

Many a people have read my words,

They flew away like morning birds.

I saw your eyes through these thin lines,

I decided they were mine.

Tricked me once that you were love and nice,

Made me feel happy, now that's twice.

All I did was admire you, three.

Now look, you did this to me.

Leave my paper to read another,

Why that sounds like scary danger.

We would not want to make me frown.

Don't you dare put me down.

If you put me down then you shall see,

What you really did to me.

But look at what I did to you.

Oh, now you want a new queue?

Tease me with desire and attention,

Did your parents fail to mention;

Not to tease people who beg please.

Oh my, don't you look unease.

Shame on me, thinking you're different.

Your eyes were so significant.

Shame on you for you made me sad.

You don't want to see me mad.

Want to know what I have done to you?

I felt your promise would fall through.

I snuck in your mind carefully,

There is no escape from me.

I said please but still you didn't listen.

So now listen to my lesson.

Eyes make promises you can't keep.

See you when we go to sleep.

The Smile in a Cloudy Day

I have curly brown hair, skin that is so smooth, and I'm pretty small.

There are thousands of me out there, but to this o ne little girl I am very special; I'm a china doll.

I was given to little Susie on her third birthday, we've been together for three years.

I've seen her small mistakes, achievements, and tears.

She talks to me every day after school and tells me about her day.

Her adventure on the money bars, she conquered the tall swirling slide, but it seems no one ever asks her to play.

Her family loves her a lot, they like to giggle with her and play pretend.

But other than me and her family, little Susie has never had a friend.

I tried to understand why this could be, she was perfect to me.

One day she ran into her room crying, as her Mom soon followed her in and had a chat: just us three.

Little Susie told her Mom how people would stare at her, and that she only felt good at home.

Her tears came pouring out as she then grabbed me and held me tight and said "Just because I have an extra, extra" she had trouble pronouncing chromosome.

Her Mom wiped her tears and told her that some people just can't see how amazing you are.

But know that your family, your doll, and I know you are the brightest star.

We all hugged and smiled as the tears faded away.

Little Susie may not be what others want to see, but she's the only person I know who finds the smile in a cloudy day.

Unspoken Word

How my thoughts stream, how they never subside.

How my dreams never seem to glide

 anymore as they peer in from the outside.

Such a feeling it is to feel so trapped inside.

Such a horrendous thing to feel nothing even when hit by sorrow's mightiest tide.

But what shall be my guide?

But how could anyone help such a soul who has an aptitude to hide.

The world never looks different when only standing on one side.

The new view you step through changes you, welcome to the ride.

Say hello to the bottomless questions others will push aside.

Say anything on your mind and soon you will find your thoughts only bide.

Emptiness has contently become my covered pride.

Emptiness and fullness somehow seem to collide.

For out of all the things in my life that have fallen through my hands one decision is left in my control, one choice left confide.

For there is only one unspoken word among me left to deicide.

Nudiustertain

I think I'm beginning to forget you, and I think I'm beginning to be okay with that.

But every time I've thought you departed you come back for a chat.

It's never about me, at least not directly.

I'm not sure how I'd react if it was, because though I look at you now it's like you can't see.

You don't see my plea for you to look at me just once the way I look at you when you're not looking.

Course maybe then the fault is mine for casting away, maybe once you looked at me that way, but I can't help wondering.

I'm missing a piece of myself that has been gone for quite some time.

Perhaps that's what you do; take pieces of people to feel better about you, and you just had to have mine.

Through the toll you put me through a switch created itself amongst the chaos you purposely drew.

This switch placed upon the missing piece turns off my emotions, time just passes in front of me, and the pain still lingers but the feelings are few.

It was nice for a while, but I must admit in my mind things felt a bit crammed.

I then realized my switch has broken; it's jammed.

And it hurts.

Joy slips through at times but only in spurts.

I can't even cry over the mourning of my own tears that won't fall out anymore.

At times I feel strong enough to lock you out, but you always seem to have a key for my door.

Your fingerprints are all over my heart.

For I can't tell where they end or the first imprint of the start.

I can't begin to explain this pain, the frustration my mind gets.

I want you to leave but the command my heart won't believe, and my mind won't forget.

I'm missing who I was yesterday more and more each day as my future self begs me to let go.

I wish these feelings were something I could handle, emotions I could show.

I will keep reaching and searching for something to hold while you're deciding whether or not I am something to hold when you are lonely.

Everything around me slips through my grip, I can feel myself beginning to drift; all I ever wanted was to be your company.

The Hidden Cherry Tree

My great aunt always spoke of a beautiful and radiant cherry tree she had found when she was little.

But she would get so frustrated with herself, for she couldn't remember where the tree was; every second she tried to solve that riddle.

My mother swore she was going crazy; she never heard the story about this tree.

I suppose I was the only one she told; the only one up for the task was me.

My withered aunt so fragile but keen sat in her wheelchair and waved goodbye as I set off for my adventure.

She couldn't remember much, but she knew it was in the Echoing Woods for sure.

With me I carried a clip board with paper and a pen.

So, every time I made a turn or hit a landmark, I could make a map of where I had been.

I started off by leaving our small town and walking along the Fox Tail River.

As I drew out the directions on the map I knew with every step, I was one more step closer.

The river leads me out to the Echoing Woods, I used to wonder how it got its name.

I soon learned that within the trees you could hear every sound; life in it was still as a picture in a frame.

I cautiously took my first steps in and embraced the view of the hundreds of tall and slim trees.

It looked as though the misty scenery went on forever; I'm not sure where the cherry tree could be.

But still I kept my faith and marked down everywhere I stepped.

I could have gone home with bad news, but that I would not accept.

And just as I was starting to lose my confidence.

I saw a gleam of light shine down; you had to be a patient adventurer for this glance.

I hurried and wrote the directions down.

Then raced back to the small town.

My aunt was still on the porch in her wheelchair as she waved to my arrival.

I ran up and placed the directions on her lap and wheeled her out as she cheered and was joyful.

She read the directions out loud as I followed.

We traveled down to the Echoing Woods to find that precious glow.

I wheeled her down the woods until we had finally made it, the sight she's been waiting to see.

Gently we stopped as she stood up from her chair and placed her hand on it and smiled while her whisper echoed, the hidden cherry tree.

"I'm much like those songs on your playlist
that you get annoyed with when they come on,
but you can't bring yourself to delete them;
it's some kind of neglected attachment.
I swear I see your eyes light up for a split second
and in that moment I'm content,
but that's not what you meant;
you were just surprised I was still around,
as I once again found,
I'm absent."

Behind the Shore

She hurt worse than a paper cut being soaked in some lemonade in May.

Why on Earth is that the only analogy I could think of to say?

Sigh.

Why?

We used to have such a love, a desire that inspired bickering people to stop and look at each other the way they used to.

Now that she's gone, her melody still lingers in my song; I have no idea what to do.

She gave me this feeling of life I had been striving to reach now it feels it was hardly in my grip.

It was never mine to keep, goodbye's she always skipped, that part was cut from my script.

She was spontaneous, often outrageous, but man was her smile contagious.

She made the sun seem dim; she was her own kind of gorgeous.

I need to forget her, every little thing I did and still adore.

It's my own fault I saw her through the harsh waves of life as a lighthouse when in reality there wasn't a place for me; I'd never meet the shore.

I didn't want her to be my Juliet.

I just wanted to live a life with her we wouldn't forget.

I didn't want her to act like a Princess; I wanted her to create herself into whatever she wanted to be.

I just thought, maybe she'd find it with me.

I thought I was the mug, and she was the coffee.

She was warm and most everyone loved her, I helped to hold her together; an embrace I guess was only felt by me.

But I can't help but miss what once filled my soul.

It's hard to accept the concept that someone who was your whole all along was trying to pull.

She pulled away, for her it was probably for the best.

At least in a way, between the layers of mistakes she's made, I was slipped in the pile for her to reach the person she was striving to be at least I'm some part of her, even if it's her past.

Now that I think of it, I can't even think of the last words she said to me were.

Maybe it's better I don't remember, I'm not sure which I prefer.

I wish I could have planned my last words better; forever my untold goodbye will be rearranged endlessly in the back of my tired mind.

For she only left her lipstick-stained coffee mug behind.

Fireplace

The midnight bells rung, as I shut the French doors.

I sighed while closing the shades, closing off from the sight of the rain that poured.

I took a sit on the ledge of the fireplace and watched the flames flicker.

My head rested on the stone above me, as the troubling thoughts in my mind grew thicker.

I thought about your smile, and then mine went away.

I imagined your touch, and how I wish you would have stayed.

To think, that I trusted you and gave you my heart.

To think, I didn't put it together that you might take me apart.

The days have grown longer, along with my thoughts.

But lately, well, these thoughts are all I've got.

See they have found a way to creep into my reality.

But these thoughts; I wish that's all I'd see.

Because along with this; I've seen the dark parts of the world you used to shelter me from.

Their shadows dissolve into my eyes as I wonder what you would think of who I've become.

I try to shake out the words you used to caress and sooth my soul with and place my mind in the right place.

For now, that you are gone, I've realized you were the darkness of the world; how well you disguised your face.

You haunt me, every single day.

You haunt me, in every possible way.

But in all do time this house will far apart.

Just like my withered heart.

These thoughts will disappear.

Someday I'll be happy you aren't here.

For now, the fireplace can keep me warm, and the crackling sound can take me away, far from my mind.

And perhaps someday again the world will be kind.

"As soon as he came in, I sank into his eyes.

He asked "Is this your first visit Miss?"

"Yes, it is my first visit anywhere""

Sollicitudo

Did you ever think you wouldn't like looking at yourself so much that you would avoid taking a shower?

Yea, me either.

I can't tell you when this all started, or frankly even why.

But I can say it hurts enough to cry.

And it sucks because I can't even seem to do that.

So, while I'm trying my best not to be a mess, my expressions are flat.

I see glimpses every now and then of who you think you see when you look at me.

Sometimes I think it'll stick around for a while, but I'm so use to this cover-up smile, it'll disappear, and I won't even notice until suddenly I feel empty.

This had been a long ongoing thing; I wish I knew the first day this sadness was found.

Maybe I was just destined to be this way, it could have accumulated until one day the flood of blues washed and drowned me inside; I'm just tried and overwhelmed with myself, as sad and dramatic as that sounds.

My head is filled with too much, too many synonyms of tragic illnesses and loud opinions; I've tried the help route, but unless you're taking up rent in a spare room up there it's hard for people to see no matter how good their intentions may be.

Everyone's advice is as good as Latin to me.

My mind is the equivalent of a dusty, horrid, neglected attic.

I have tried to climb the stairs in attempt to tidy up, but I only ever get in a few steps until I leave in a panic.

Those top steps have been layered in dust for ages.

A layer for every time I jump out of my valiant absent phases.

I confess this is my mess, I am so afraid of everything and I can't explain how overwhelmingly exhausted I am.

I could guess what you're thinking, what could possibly be so wrong with me; this is one heck of a dramatic scam.

But the truth is there are heavily labeled boxes up in this scattered mind.

There was a day, a time, where I could move them, but their weight has increased since then; and back then I didn't feel confined.

The weight pushes down on me so hard lately, almost to the point where I don't want to move at all and I'm letting things slip away.

I don't want them to, I try to move, but my muscles have cut off connections, my vocal cords agree with no objection, it's my heart that stings as it feels the things I love detach and part ways.

What am I without the ones I love who care for me unconditionally even when they don't know what I'm holding in.

What if one day when I look around, I won't hear a single sound except for my knees when they hit the ground, because I have been forgotten?

What if they're happy without me?

What if that's what I don't see?

I don't believe this is so but what do I know; I do know that if it came down to it and my absence would bring them bliss then so be it.

I'd pack my bags and start counting my long days, they mean that much to me; if without me would make them happy then it's time to forget.

Because if they're happy, then a piece of me is happy and maybe one day it will conquer the part of me that can't find happiness anymore.

The flood will pass on, I could joyfully sing along to happy songs, maybe I could even finally reach the attic door.

A part of me believes I don't deserve to have these thoughts.

I've never known how to say that, in my throat it always gets caught.

Other people are struggling, and I should be helping, not constantly thinking of this negativity, a constant streaming brainwave station:

'You're on with MDD and Anxiety coming at you live on the air!' but I have to say it's not fair to try and continuously repair your own foundation.

As odd as it may sound, I think a part of me cut town.

A part of me shutdown.

It's gone it left; I didn't even get to say my goodbyes.

I don't know where it could be, maybe still lingering, or off somewhere in the free-spirited air; flying in the wind with them are our cut ties.

Maybe that's why I'm sad majority of the time.

I'm mourning, that part of me that's gone, and I have anxiety from waiting for it to come back and I am terrified it will never come back and I am living in a hopeless sublime.

In this wait I sit.

Not knowing if any second it will return, or everyday I'm growing further and further away from it.

I used to be the adventurous one you know.

Course I can't blame you for thinking no, I know it doesn't show.

Not everyone can be the wild one.

Sometimes I come to peace with that, but just once in a while I want to be the one who really lived when the day is done.

Oh, how I miss my younger self, but even just trying to reach back it's a struggle to hold everything together.

It could be just me, or the little circles I've been conformed to rely on lying to me; my own memories and stories are hard to remember.

I want to call it quits; I can't handle this plotted tragic.

But as much as I may want to, that just won't do because I know this to be true; there is a light on in this attic.

One day I'm going to climb up those stairs and the world had better be prepared because I will be no longer scared; because from that point on I have seen the worst within me and I am letting it go, I will finally be free to roam.

And maybe my past self won't come back but I'll find a new me to fill the empty gaps of my soul with a cozy warmth it lacks; and perhaps then my long-lost piece will feel my peace and come back to call me home.

I have battles to face but I'll make it there, one day at a time, one step, one stair; I will not be defined of these thoughts that invaded and over welcomed their stay.

I am just a person who had a bad day.

Adrift Static

G: "Hello?"

B: "Um, yes hello, how did you get in my radio?"

G: "Radio- I picked up this old phone and it just started to ring?"

B: "Well I was listening to my favorite show and your voice started to grow; isn't this a peculiar thing?"

G: "You're listening to a show, I've never heard of that?"

B: "Why yes, you must have an awfully boring time, no wonder you were looking for a chat."

G: "I just moved into this house, so I decided to explore and behind the attic door I found this old pone just waiting to be used."

B: "You sound too young to be moving yourself, I'm confused."

G: "Well I moved here with my Dad; do you have any family?"

B: "A small one as well, just me and my folks; perhaps when I'm older I'll have a family of my own, but if not that's fine with me."

G: "You're lucky to have a Mother."

B: "Why, what happened to her?"

G: "She left when I was little, I don't remember."

B: "If I had a son or daughter, I would never leave him or her."

G: "My Dad never left me."

B: "It's okay to have a small family."

G: "My Dad, I think he loves me but, he's just always busy."

B: "Maybe he just has a lot to do to get everything for you, but I'm positive he loves you."

G: "Grownups are always in such a hurry."

B: "I never want to be like that, I just want to make people happy."

G: "I think you may be from the past, and maybe I'm in the future."

B: "Well if that's the case I hope things get better."

B: "I just feel really sad."

G: "So is my Dad."

G: "I wish it would go away; I feel like he'll be sad forever."

B: "I'm sure you make him happy just being his daughter."

G: "I like talking to you."

B: "You make me smile too."

G: "I think I have to go though; my Dad is calling me."

B: "I fear if you hang up, we won't be able to reach each other again, and boldly I must say you improved my reality."

G: "If we can't, I know my Dad has an old radio, maybe I can try to talk to you on there?"

B: "Okay, okay I'll keep it forever just in case you come back, I swear!"

G: "I hope I get to talk to you again, and someday you'll be happy."

B: "I hope you have a good day, a good life, and your Dad finds happiness he can see."

G: "I guess I should say goodbye even though I don't want to."

B: "Wait- before you do, can I know your name I don't want to forget you."

G: "My name is Marie, I'm sorry I have to go my Dad's calling me!"

B: "Just, one more thing I'm sorry;"

B: "Goodbye for now, and remember, Marie, tomorrow can be your anything."

G: "Hey, my Dad says the same thing-"

Rorrim

The mirror is foggy I cannot see.

See I cannot mirror the fogginess within me.

My mind is backwards, and I can't think straight.

Straight and backwards can't function in my mind they need to separate.

When did I get up, I thought I was lying down, how can this be?

Because when I thought I was down I was seen as up; people choose what they see.

What's in it for me when I wipe my hand across this glass?

Glass that looks so trusting but dares to uncover the shudder of the disgusting realities I wish to leave undiscovered, I'll keep my hand down but it's tempting every time I pass.

The fog how it mocks me silently.

Silently it creeps through the thick silence I've purposely casted in hopes it will trick the fog but it's far cleverer than I thought, it won't go away easily.

I can't outsmart it, and it's growing darker.

Darker than the growing hole in my soul that only I know; only an acquaintance for now but I don't care to go much farther.

Asking for help won't help at all.

All it will bring are stirred questions and complicated endings, even if I wanted to make my one call from this prison, I call my heart's walls who could I tell who wouldn't just end it in yells, it's hard to help someone who's halfway through the fall.

And so, I am alone, and as so it is better this way I think, I just need to think.

Think of a way to unmask this monster that lurks amongst unfamiliar silence, I am categorized as prey, my joints feel locked, and I've been staring so long it hurts to blink.

I want to move on, but that seems so hard to do.

Do I move on from what I'm used to, or stay for the sake of comfort in routines and lack of redoes?

No, I need to stop this; this has gone on long enough.

Enough with all this backwards talk of straight and narrow paths I have no intention of traveling, it's so hard to want to move when your mind is filled with tough and heavy stuff.

I can't stop thinking about the glass.

The glass, no it's not the glass I'm thinking of the fog, the fog; I need an escape, an overpass.

Only I can save myself.

It won't unmask itself.

My hand is shaking as I raise it up, my reflection can't even be seen amongst the fog's thick darkness.

Darkness has cluttered my mind for such a long time, goodness have I created quite the mess.

It's time to clean it up.

Up my hand goes, the scene is setup.

First my fingertips meet its cold touch, but they don't retreat, they glide making room for my palm for a moment I feel stuck.

Stuck in this little pocket of time that has neither consequence nor reason, and for once that sounds nice, I will no longer stand by in this darkness of ruck.

In one swift movement my hand is sent across this fog that has tried to define me, a divide I can see, bliss covers my mind at the thought of moving on and changing.

Changing, what an interesting point of view, indeed now I can look right through, but defining me I guess was true, for I see nothing.

Now is the Hour

I've roamed this home alone, for the past fifteen years.

Everyday feels like the evening you drifted off from me and the world we had both faced throughout the fear and tears.

Our children swing by every now and then to make an appearance.

And it's nice to see how much they have grown and how proud they have made us both, but still, I feel the distance.

The distance between me and the world.

The pain and agony of not hearing you call me your girl.

I've been told to let go of my pain, and it will help me through.

But my Dear I fear I am losing you more each day, more each day it becomes so real, that the pain I feel is the closest thing I have to you.

And as I walk now to our old record player,

My hands shake, grabbing onto Bing Crosby's venial with your favorite "Now Is the Hour".

The crisp tenor voice swept through the echoing halls, making them young again.

And as the record slowly spun, I began to twirl with it, pretending to dance with you as we used to back then.

While my hands gripped onto the air, I closed my eyes.

My feet began to turn, but they turned too fast for my old legs, as a pain shot up from my feet to my thighs.

I felt my withered body begin to fall, as Bing's voice still sweetly sang around me.

I felt my arms reach to grab onto something, I imagined I was falling into the sea.

But soon enough I hit the wood floor.

My glasses shattered around me along with a bump on my head as blood slowly poured.

But to my surprise it didn't hurt, I didn't even cry.

Bing softly sings "Now is the hour when we must say goodbye."

I felt a great deal of my pain was lifting off my shoulders; I was done growing older, as I began to smile, for you came to rescue me from this fear.

You slid your hands in mine helping me up on my feet, as you sang the last words with the record "When you return, you'll find me waiting here."

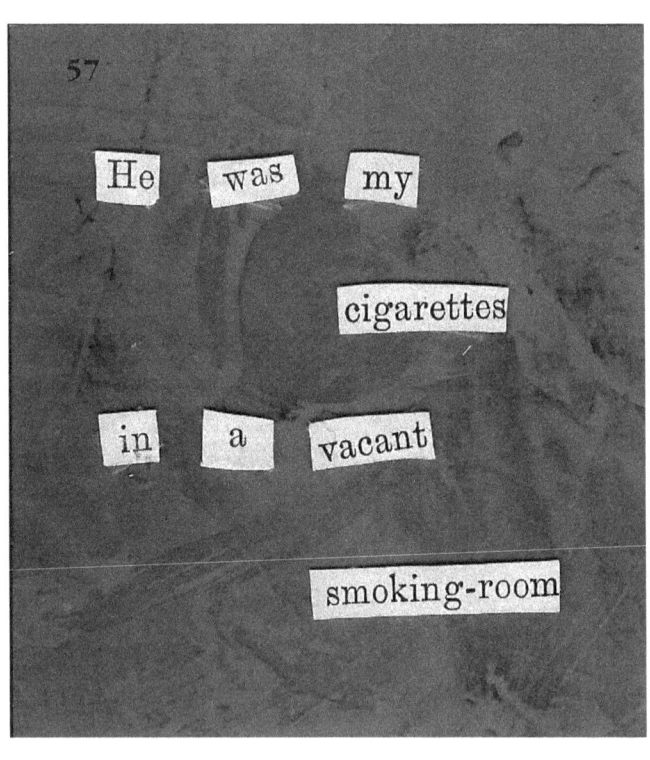

Faded Tapes

Our film stopped spinning.

Our picture has stopped developing.

You wandered from the frame.

Still, I tried to act the same.

But I can't read a script written for two.

This just doesn't seem like you.

I'll hold my place and wait for your return.

With faded colors bleeding in from previous tapes; you'd think by now I'd learn.

That I can't grasp onto colors that weren't meant for me.

I always imagine you stepping back in, but that I never see.

Now left in the black room, my only company is the negatives on the floor.

Because you tapped over me when I wasn't entertaining anymore.

The Binding Myth

She was his hero, though he was the one on the battlefield.

Thousands of miles apart, and over time, only brought together by letters written with love and neatly sealed.

She kept herself busy in her days of solitude by painting in the sunroom.

Every time she began a painting it had the potential of joy but ended in gloom.

While he traveled along with his fellow soldiers, he often thought of how she must be doing.

He hated the thought that he and his love were both under the same sky, but still, he couldn't hold her to stop the crying.

Each letter written by her was neatly creased and sent along with a pressed flower.

The cold nights he had to bear would have consumed him, if it wasn't for her.

Each letter written by him he wrote a small poem on the bottom of the page.

He wrote of their unbinding love, and how her work would someday make the stage.

Every time he stepped onto the field; he carried a picture of her in his pocket.

And every time she left the house, she wore her wedding locket.

A myth is told that when your other half is in pain or has to be checking out, time seems to stop.

She halted in the middle of the sidewalk with a sharp pain in her chest, as he fell, with the photo of her beginning to drop.

Her hand shot up to her locket as she held the cold silver in her palm.

The photo had finally floated to the ground, he tried to stay calm.

Tears ran down her face, and softly she prayed to herself in the midst of the busy world.

The single last tear he would have to shed ran down his face as his last breath escaped, the photo by his side, he smiled goodbye to his only girl.

"Oh she was a risky girl with a broken heart. So tonight the world was going to fall apart."

The Outside People

I'm ugly, but oh that's okay, for I get to see the things the beautiful cannot.

They often overlook what my breath took the most delightful of a spot.

Beauty itself shot straight up from the filth in which they never bother to look down and see.

Such an indelicate neglect, the shamefulness to forget, taken for granted nature that surrounds us; it never passes me.

I'm ugly, but oh that's okay, for I get to feel things the beautiful cannot.

As they pass me by along the street, bumping shoulders as we meet; though I am left distraught for me to cross their mind it isn't given a thought.

I get to feel the genuine kindness of another; I get to feel the true beauty of a soul.

They will waste away in front of countless mirrors as I continue my interrupted stroll.

I'm ugly, but oh that's okay, for I get to touch things the beautiful cannot.

They may marvel at the things they have bought, but I know something they haven't been taught; I have something they haven't got.

As for the rest just like me we get to see the world for what it's meant to be, the touch of beautiful life dripped on the canvas upon our easel.

You all have the same reflection, until you peel away the fake complexion and stop reaching for perfection; you can call us the outside people.

"Now I hate this top floor window,

with its old white paint peeling.

For it had a perfect view of you leaving."

Obscurity of Animosity

I'm told to love myself, and I can't find the motivation to.

But I'll find little reasons to try and pull it off for you.

Because really that's what you want to see, because if I smile and look fine that's what I'll portray to be.

When I'm alone and the dark is more comforting, more relatable, then the people outside that's when I truly see.

I see the person beyond the outer layer of my skin, buried deep under the piles of sin, lurking behind the shadows I've tried to cast away.

They insist to stay, so there in the depths of my soul they lay.

I can't shoo them out, they have no other place to go.

I've relied on them too much; I can't remember a time where I wasn't this low.

This is one heck of a long running show I have been giving, and I must applaud those who came into the business of life without a harsh curtain fall.

For I can't even recall the last moment in time I felt happy with myself in my own little world; I'm not sure what it would be called.

Planet for the melodramatic: a place for the tireless to rest and a spot for the lonesome to gather.

Maybe it's just a place we can kick it for a while until we find our smile, until such a thing comes to existence, I guess it really doesn't matter.

Because through my eyes I will always be the person who didn't measure up and didn't stand a chance.

And at my expense, no offense, I hardly think it matters enough to say out loud; we all have our own demons wrapped in flaws, some see them in awe, but only at a glance.

The thought of love sounds lovely.

The thought is what I've got, and for a while I think it'll be enough; from the last encounter with said lover, love just isn't the scene for me.

Speaking of love, it sounds like you have something to say.

I've heard this before, now I have a question coming your way.

Do you think that you could love a total stranger, even if you tried really hard and put down your guard?

If your answer is no, then I'm afraid your hypocrite side is showing, for telling me to love myself; now there's your final applaud.

"Come meet me at the hidden train tracks,

we'll make our run for it and find something new.

There's a world out there waiting for us,

and I must say

I wouldn't want to find it with anyone but you."

She was Enough

She was a normal child, and he was her friend.

Only coming into existence when her eyes closed, lying in bed.

As she drifted away from everything she didn't understand, there he stood, smiling, ready for anything.

Anything her imagination wished; they were off until morning.

He would wait for her, somewhere in the back of her mind.

She would run to him at the end of the day, because people aren't always kind.

So even though it all may not be real, the time spent with him made her feel special, and okay when she awoke.

And if ever during the day she was sad, she remembered and replayed all the words he spoke.

He told her she was enough and that she always would be.

Even if she found she didn't always need him he would be there for her, she just had to look and see.

Years went by for her, for him it only felt like moments slipping by.

She told him of the world she saw; he could see it in her glistening eyes.

The visits became less frequent.

He didn't know where she went.

Did he ever cross her mind, was she okay?

He hoped it was so, but he didn't know, this increasingly small part of her mind is where he was to stay.

And that he did, keeping his promise.

To always be there, despite all the things he'll miss.

How they flew Hot Air Balloons to the ocean just so they could skip rocks.

Before they left, so she could catch the morning light, they would jump off the dock.

Missing the way, the sun shined when she was near.

Missing, waiting, wait- he is interrupted in his thoughts; someone is here.

It felt like ages since he heard something, adjusting his eyes from the darkness he had grown use to, to a bright blur.

Smiling at the sight, so lovely and bright, it was her.

Her smile didn't reflect his though, she was more surprised.

"You're still here?" Her question echoed through all their memories, and his time spent waiting; his heart felt incised.

Just barley he nodded; he still couldn't believe his eyes.

All this time he thought she must be dreaming of someone else, but she found him, and he was ready to run around or take to the skies.

Gently taking her by the hand, excited to run into their next journey; she was his joy, his light, his pith.

But she didn't move, she wasn't going with.

Turning around as her hand slipped out of his, his light he hadn't noticed had a crack.

She was leaving, and not coming back.

But he couldn't leave, for him there was no door.

Things weren't so lovely and bright anymore.

She was still somewhere; she would be able to hear; he had just a few moments until she found the morning.

She was his missing piece, his best friend, his only memory; he had to think of something.

He felt her leaving as the darkness found its way back to him; what could he say to make her stay, he didn't know.

"I'm not ready for our adventures to end, please, please I don't want you to wake up, please don't go-"

Broken Strings

I've loved with all my soul, and I've repaired it on my own.

I have been left to take the unraveled thread that had closed the cracks on my heart and take new string to what I have already tried to sew.

My steps have gotten heavier, along with the burdens on my shoulders.

Love is supposed to be such a beautiful, timeless pleasure; but its acts are getting repetitive, and I am getting older.

With every task I do I feel you slip through the cracks of my thoughts.

I always feel ashamed, for you must have forgotten about me, but unfortunately the harsh lessons are imprinted in my head that you taught.

I wish I could take back all the minutes I spent with you, all the laughter and memories.

For they come back and haunt me in my dreams.

My reality has distorted itself into such a colorless thing.

Leaving me here in wonder and heart ache, with my broken strings.

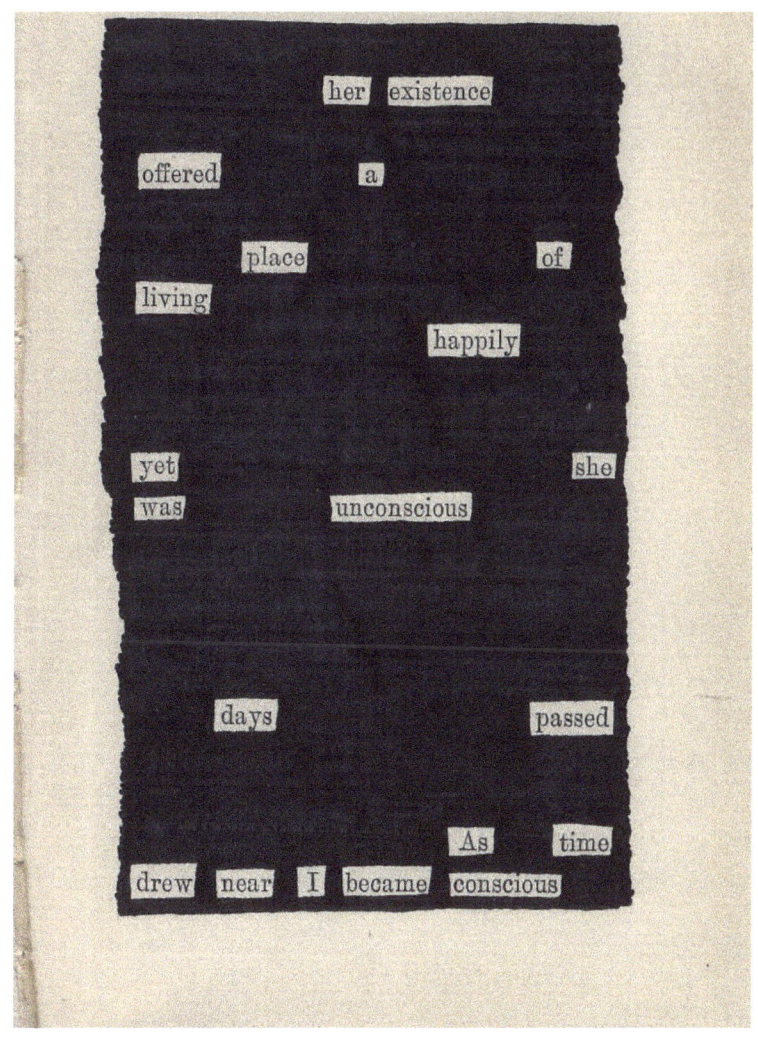

"Her existence offered a place of living happily, yet she was unconscious.

Days passed, as time drew near, I became conscious."

Him & Her

Dialing the number, he could feel his heartbeat in his chest as it rang; hearing a noise he wasn't expecting.

She had actually answered, at first, he felt flattered, but she probably only did to stop the voice mails she had been collecting.

Him: Hey

Her: Hi, now go away

Him: I made a living will today, it was the most boring thing I've ever done

Her: Well doesn't that sound like fun

Him: I thought you'd say something like that

Her: Look, is there a certain reason you wanted so badly to chat?

Him: I just kind of miss you, that's all

Her: Yea I can kinda tell with all the calls

Him: Why didn't you answer?

Her: Why did you choose her?

Him: Are we really still on that again?

Her: If you wanted to move passed it, you could just answer then

Him: I was foolish

Her: You were selfish

Him: I know, and I don't deserve your trust, your touch

Her: You really screwed up, I used to admire you so much

Him: Do you still, because you I will always adore

Her: No, not really anymore

Him: I suppose I can't blame you, I should have been better, I should have cleaned up my intent, for you were a blessing I was so lucky to have been sent

Her: Its things like that, that make me wonder where you went

Him: I'm still here, and I will be everyday

Her: That's too fast, you can't say things like that, I can't get over what you've done to my past, and it's not okay

Him: Okay, I didn't really mean it anyway

Her: I was gonna say, that's cliché

Him: Oh…

Her: So…

Him: So, I guess I shouldn't have called you

Her: It's not the first time, it seems like a new hobby you do

Him: Well just forget about me then why don't you?!

Her: Looks like there's nothing new

Him: What's that supposed to mean?

Her: It's either a pity party with you or a messed-up parade, there's literally no in-between

Him: You always knew how to keep me grounded

Her: I'm not gonna lie, I miss the way your words sounded

Him: I wish I could see you

Her: You know that's something we can't do

Him: But I thought you missed me, what did I say?

Her: Nothing, okay?

Him: No it's clearly something

Her: It really isn't anything!

Him:

Her: I just don't really want to talk

Him: Wanna go for a walk?

Her: That's not what I meant; I mean I don't know what to say to you

Him: Yea me too

Her: I don't get you, there, that's what it is, I don't understand you

Him: Me too-

Her: We can't be together, and you know that, why do you keep doing this?

Him: It's just, when I wake up, I always forget for a moment that we're no longer together, and I can't get over that; it's just something I'll always miss

Her: Every week it's the same ordeal, I need to move and carry on with my life you aren't healthy for me, let me go!

Him: But you're everything I know…

Her: You're going to find someone; I know you will

Him: Without you though my life just feels still

Her: I was done waiting a long time ago

Him: I know

Her: We should probably just head to bed

Him: Yea, I'll probably do that and take my meds

Her: Good, now go get some sleep

Him: See how I remembered to take my medicine just like you used to do, you always used to get so upset when I'd forget but now it's something, I'll always keep

Her: I'm glad you remember that, it's important

Him: I really wish I could see you and make it all up to you and tell you all the things I really meant

Her: Goodbye now

Him: Please, please don't hang up I can't move on I don't know how!

Her: I'm sorry

Him: No, no please don't be

Her: This is for the best, you just don't understand

Him: I can try to, please I just need you, I miss holding your hands

Her: You're hurting me, this all hurts me too you know, just stop and get out!

Him: There's no need to shout!

Her: This is the last time, I have to go, please, please sleep; goodbye

Him: I just want to be your only guy

Her: It's time to go.

Him: But I,- H- Hello?

Mistaken Music

Our love reigned like music; music that danced about my life.

With such great-hearted heaviness, you can only imagine the pain when it falls, the sharpness of a knife.

The deafening ringing in my ears, from the loss of our melody.

Still at times just faintly I hear a few soft notes; lingering reprises of you and me.

You caught me off guard; you pulled me when my world began to totter.

You held me; I was just lost in your essence to realize I was under water.

But the refrain could still be heard, despite the fact I was submerged.

Not seeing you were above the reflecting waves, slowly you unmerged.

I thought I was surrounded by your grace.

Lost in the alluring vagueness of your face.

Once your grip released, as I floated to the top.

Seeing you throw our sheets of music in the shore, I wished for you to stop.

I wished for the music to chime once again.

But it's time I compose notes of my own, though our notes are tossed in now and then.

I don't want someone to come and save me, I want to be the one.

I want to save myself, in the long run it's just me when all is done.

Though without their shared notes, I couldn't have created this music of my own, for now it dances about itself.

It's time I fall in love with myself.

Technicolor Dance

My soul peaked upon a canvas in which I only showed to you.

You seemed to be the only person who didn't see right through.

Through the tattered, matted, faded, twisted linen that pressed my flaws away.

Instead, you embraced them, as I have tried in the past; through my doubt you stayed.

Ever so gently you stroked new colors over the dark and washed-out ones someone carelessly painted before.

How could I know once you had started, I would live for the moment you painted more.

Distracted by the beauty of every move you made.

I couldn't make a move after you tore a hole through the canvas; still I wish you had stayed.

A tear slashed through the middle of the bright burst of color, I didn't see your plan.

How I begged for Technicolor, but you barely kicked over, in pitied mercy, a black paint can.

Toddled over, the darkness engulfed what was left of the faint color; the burden to suffocate.

Even worse to see the artist who isn't fazed by their own raze; all the familiar feelings of betrayal begin to intoxicate.

And now it hurts to swallow, and now it hurts to breathe.

It hurts to sleep on my scars I now hide underneath.

I am losing my faith, slowly and steadily.

I've always thought of the ending, but I've never really been ready.

And why do my demons only ask for a dance when my feet sore?

Can't they see I don't know how to dance anymore?

I used to believe that I needed you.

Pity I didn't see you never needed me, but if not you then who is the question I'm left to.

Save all of this, I should be the one making the apology.

For I am terribly sorry, you thought, you knew me.

Uncharted

I walked out the door to the garage, wearing the light blue shirt you said reminded you of the sky on its best days.

I'll always love and remember the way you made small things seem just as important, and how you could never look bad in any way.

As I reached behind me, shutting the door, while my eyes were stuck on the beat-up red car we saved up for and bought years ago.

A single thought crossed my mind, as I got in, but I had no place to go.

I thought of your precious and selfless smile, starting up the engine.

Putting it in park, relaxing back, as thoughts of your absent affection and perfection tried to calm my adrenaline.

With a little flick of my finger, I locked the doors.

With a little reaction I felt my anxiousness escape through my pores.

Now all I have to do is breath, you wouldn't believe the things I have yet to tell you.

How it used to be so hard to inhale, exhaling seemed like something new.

Our memories will carry me through until I feel myself drop to a stop.

Remember our long talks on the roof top?

Talking up wishes and plans to travel and explore.

They are left uncharted; although I can still imagine our thoughts I've desperately wanted more.

I know this is something you wouldn't want.

But you must admit I have made it far for a soul without a north star, a soul left in a haunting gaunt.

If you were slipped into my shoes, being how strong you are, you wouldn't do this to yourself.

Left in this world without you, I don't want to one day have to sing happy birthday to myself.

This scent has intertwined my lungs, closing my eyes as the engine hums, our last uncharted ride.

Your voice, it calls me home; softly pulled to the other side.

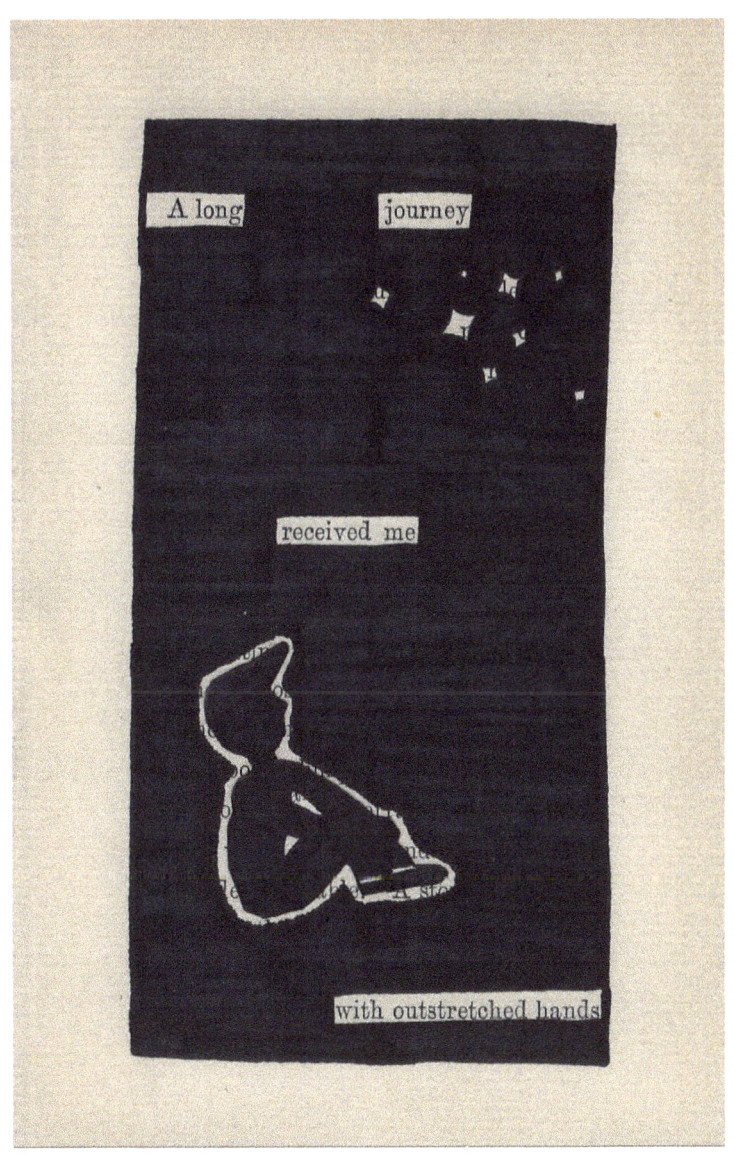

"A long journey received me with outstretched hands."

Her Dance

I stare upon the floor, and then look up to her face.

Her face that glows so heavenly, even in this darkest place.

Inhaling the smug air in and embracing myself to stand.

My legs straighten out as my knees unbuckle, and I searched to reach her hand.

I slipped my hand in the palm of hers, gently grasping it between my fingers.

Holding the most delicate creation in my arms, away from all harm, all that echoes my mind is her.

Her and her graceful dancing, filling the room around us with the soft elegance of her voice.

She sang songs of love, for through her eyes I was her only choice.

My eyes began to close as my body unconsciously was still swaying.

I hadn't known a touch of love until she became a part of me; I hadn't even known the feeling of dancing.

The warmth of her body kept me going, along with her refusal of defeat.

With the blissful thoughts traveling and creating a smile on my face, I tripped over my own feet.

I fell onto the hardwood floor as the sound pondered the room and drowned out the sound of the music, I scattered quickly to help and find her.

But yet again my mind deceives me; it was nothing but the smug air between my fingers.

"I'll be your grand adventure.

You'll be my strong protector.

Call me your defender.

You can be my last surrender."

Ordinarily Common

He was an ordinarily common man, as was his life.

He would never change a thing, but to see her smile once again, his long-missed wife.

She left him in the spring.

She finally joined the birds and released her wings.

Though she didn't want to leave it was time for her to go.

Though he knows he should leave this house where he still hears all her hellos, he cannot seem to part, it hurts his heart; now it's already beginning to snow.

They used to watch movies together when it was this cold.

They hadn't thought of this plot; one young forever, the other to grow lonely and old.

Lonely for the ordinary he didn't mind, as he looked to his trembling fingers, oh how they used to dance, and they twirled.

Lonely, now to hold his own hand with its tremors and he can't find the strength to stand; but that was him just trying to understand the world.

Not a thing of hers was moved.

Not that it needed to be improved.

With her things left in its place sometimes around corners he'd catch a glimpse of her face.

With the youth left in his legs he'd chase his own haze, hoping for an embrace, but her shadow he can never seem to trace.

Everything will be okay, everyone said.

Everything would be fine if it was her words instead.

But his mind is slipping, how he grows upset.

But he isn't ready, he doesn't want to forget.

Still, he replaces the flowers in her vase, each time they die it's like saying goodbye to her all over again; as he pours new water in and watching it as it swirled.

Still as the resting stems, he watches them, but that was him just trying to understand the world.

Tired, he's become.

Tired of pain from not feeling the same, his Doctors can't medicate the emotions that have gone numb.

All he does is wait for the day he'll finally fly away.

All he's ever wished is to go out when he insists; perhaps he'll leave in the sun of May.

People around him wish he wouldn't talk like this.

People dismiss the pain he feels without one half of him; the half every day is missed.

The sun is out, and the flowers are blooming; he's told he should be happy.

The clock is ticking slowly, gladly he'll smile for it won't be that long of awhile; he won't be missed that badly.

To his closet he went one last time, slipping her sweater on, why she had to leave so soon before he didn't know but he's coming home; climbing in bed, in the blankets he curled.

To the Earth he said goodbye, but it didn't cry for the ordinarily common guy; a man who tried his best to understand the world.

The Colorful Shelter

Paint me a different sky they said, and so I did.

I gave them all the colors I had, even the ones after all these years I hid.

The more colors they commanded to be splattered on their palate, the more washed out I became.

Until one day their eyes drifted off their own colorful world and onto mine, forgetting I helped them make that sky; they left because I wasn't the same.

I wasn't the person they claimed to be in love with before.

They wore the vibrant colors proud; their pride was so loud, the ones that once consumed me and they adored.

The only colors I seem to be able to mix and scrap up these days are blacks and grays.

There's only so much I can think while looking into these; the sadness that over welcomes its stay.

My eyes adjust deeply into this sea surrounding me, a void of a comfortable black.

In this darkness I get lost in so many thoughts it's hard to keep on track.

While searching for the light inside of me, this is the only time I feel free.

And that's when I find you, but only for a second, sometimes you're out of reach; but I will come back, stay with me.

Stay inside and remind me you are there, that someday you'll be my outer cover, but for now you're my soul's shelter.

Someday again I will paint a sky for just you and I, my unstained colors.

All I wanted was for you to look at me like I was the only girl in the world,
    but
you looked at everyone in the world but me

Alive

-What I'm trying to say, is I think we're gonna be okay,

I think we're gonna make it around to the final round.

And this feeling isn't going to win even if we have to wing it,

We'll do it together because things just have to get better.

This isn't our plot,

We're not gonna rot,

In this place of restless-heartless sadness,

I'll find your hand in your thick darkness.

I'll step over my own mess and I promise,

I'll show you a sunrise.

And I'll prove to you the prize you are,

Because you are my North Star,

And our happiness isn't that far.

No, not at all,

I can see it over this wall.

You and I are going to thrive,

And I swear we're not going to just survive.

I will show you the heartbeat of completely being alive.

Pretty Girls

Pretty girls laugh, even when there's nothing to laugh at, at all.

Pretty girls don't make themselves feel small.

Pretty girls stand tall.

Pretty girls don't fall.

Pretty girls smile wide.

Pretty girls don't try to hide.

Pretty girls have a proud Mom and Dad.

Pretty girls aren't sad.

Pretty girls have dry eyes.

Pretty girls don't cry.

Pretty girls have no one to trick.

Pretty girls don't make themselves sick.

Pretty girls don't have to make wishes on stars.

Pretty girls don't have scars.

Pretty girls can always laugh.

Pretty girls don't die, they live through their photographs.

"She was an eternal fall, and he was uncoordinated and blue.

His world was settled and on time, and she was long overdue."

Adventure of Life

With every breath that flowed in me, I felt the adventure pulse through my body.

Every day was something new, with the most beautiful gal beside me.

Neither of us were afraid of anything that came our way.

How could we let fear control the path of our day?

We had albums upon albums of the captured moments of our journeys.

But don't get me wrong, we had our fair share of worries.

My Love and I had fights, and troubles that followed for quite some years.

Soon the adventures had to stop; a whole new life would appear.

We got use to a life of busy schedules and loose change.

I missed the adrenalin rush, instead of the stock exchange.

The calendars went by, along with our young heartfelt dreams.

The only adventures we had now were our daily walks together by the stream.

She longed for a family of our own, but we ran into problems.

We never did get to fill all those empty slots in our picture albums.

But all in time the days grew longer, and life was getting shorter.

I found my old self stumbling upon old memories, walking alone by the water.

We didn't have a fear in the world, but now it has consumed me.

I long for the day where I feel no pulse go through this frail body.

Once in a while I look through me and my Love's old pictures and silently reminisce.

I used to yearn for adventure, but now it's just her smile I miss.

I was prepared for everything that came by me; I thought I could handle the strife.

But I failed to see I was nowhere near prepared for my biggest adventure, life.

Sheepish Tryst

"I swear this lecture hall will be the death of me."

'Time for another two-hour monotone speech, I wonder what today will be.'

"I suppose things could be worse, instead of a mumbling unenthused professor I could have, whelp nope, that's about it."

'This class of 500 people wouldn't be half bad if these small, bolted to the floor chairs actually made it comfortable to sit.'

"At least I don't really know anyone, and if I wanted to skip the professor wouldn't even know I wasn't here."

'I wonder if anyone even knows I'm there or hardly cares.'

"It's been a few weeks into the class, and there's really only one thing I find interesting."

'I keep coming to class because there's a lass a few seats down from me; she's the most brilliant excuse for daydreaming.'

"I didn't let him see that I knew he stole glances at me; I can't lie it's kind of adorable."

'She sat cross-legged in these God forsaken chairs, I don't know how she does it, she makes it look so bearable.'

"He seems all together in a messy kind of way, sometimes I pray for rainy days, so he wears his cute yellow coat."

'She doodled flowers in the margins of her neglected notes.'

"He's something like a paradox."

'Her jeans were always rolled up a few cuffs above the ankle, always showing off her socks.'

"There just has to be plenty of mysteries within him to unlock."

'Gosh she loved her odd little socks.'

"I wonder what his major is, or is he as lost as me?"

'Her hair, for a while, was like walls covering the side profile view of her face; so for a while she was a mystery, until one day she tucked her insecurity behind her ear, uncovering this sophisticated face but gosh was I wrong, she still very well was a mystery.'

"It's been a few months and we've daringly stolen a few smiles from one another."

'Her smile makes my day; gosh I really would love to talk to her.'

"Would he think it's weird if I sometimes imagined there was no one else in this lecture hall, oh yea sure not at all; no, it's weird, I'm just going to assume."

'Maybe it's weird, but sometimes it felt like we were the only two in the whole room.'

"His style made me smile like a giddy geek."

'I can't tell if she likes my clothes, or she thinks I'm a freak.'

"Goodness his scarf collection was impressively and adorably endless."

'I hate to be cocky, but I think she may like me; her essence seemed so timeless.'

"I've thought of starting a conversation about his tattoos, but he always leaves class so quickly."

'A few times she even wore a loose bowtie, which I can't lie caught me by surprise but my did she pull it off quite awesomely.'

"Besides his presence this dreaded lecture hall held some kind of use."

'If I was ever called out for not paying attention, though she is guilty of the conviction, I would never throw her to the accused.'

"Though it takes a while for everyone to pile out I wait for all these rows of chairs to empty until it's just me, for then it is the perfect place to read."

'Today after class was let out, I decided to wait outside the door for her, my awkward self will start up some kind of conversation, maybe then she'll take the lead.'

"Ah yes, perfectly quiet."

'I wonder where she could be, this is her closest exit.'

"Not a sound, not a murmur."

'Maybe I'll be able to catch her tomorrow, but while passing the open door my eyes couldn't help but explore; it's her.'

"Just me and my book, I can't wait to get past these next few chapters."

'Oh my gosh she loves to read too, that's adorable, I'm going to ninja-like sneak up and surprise her.'

"Placing my finger on the page I lifted my head to feel a surprised expression cover my face; it was him, sitting cross-legged on the table ahead of me."

'I could finally see her straight on, the suspension is gone, and I think she'd agree.'

"He smiled for a moment more, and with a crack in his voice at first that we both giggled at, he asked me if I came here often."

'Really that's what we're going with, oh my gosh I'm an idiot, I might as well hand her some nails and a hammer for my awkward coffin.'

"The first thing he did was make me laugh; I don't even mind that he interrupted my reading."

'Wait she didn't blow me off she's, she's laughing.'

"I discreetly closed my book, and we began small talking about how boring our professor's teaching was, and how finals are gonna suck."

'She's so easy to talk to, this doesn't feel new; it feels genuine and true, this is quite some luck.'

"We decided to go for a walk, it's nice outside."

'As we walked, from the corner of my eye I saw her tuck her hair behind her ear; she doesn't have to hide.'

"He was dorky."

'She was quirky.'

"I can't help but ponder over the wonder of what in the world he must see in me."

'I wonder how big her smile could grow to be; I hope one day I get the pleasure to see.'

"We both seemed kind of out of place in this big campus population."

'This little walk felt like a new rotation, like we were on our way to a mini vacation to get away from the expectation of college education; I'll be the navigation as she points to the destination of perhaps a new foundation.'

"I don't know why right now I don't feel as shy, but I like this feeling."

'We kept smiling and talking, she's such a pleasure to be with even just simply walking.'

"What if eventually he sees what I'm afraid I am?"

'She kind of stopped walking, I wasn't sure why, but I could see something got to her, like we had a telepathic telegram.'

"I shouldn't have come on this walk he isn't going to like me; I don't want to get hurt."

'She even looked cute while she was puzzled, as she gently kicked some rocks that strolled from the dirt.'

"I like him, I do, I'm just afraid, I un-tucked my hair; I'm too nervous to talk."

'I smiled at her action and to my reaction; lightly I tucked her hair back, smiled, and told her I liked her socks.'

"Surprised by his actions my eyes drew to his and without a single word he made me feel warm and safe, maybe I was okay."

'Her smile could literally save the world, and yea that sounds stupid and childish but right now my only wish is to show her that maybe it wouldn't change the *world*, but it would definitely change mine; she just makes my day.'

"Perhaps an awkward girl and a somewhat shy, charming guy could make it together in this world or at least we'd give it a try."

'I think her smile just sealed my heart, we were like some piece of revived lost art; my daydreams no longer have to occupy my wandering mind, she can be my ironically adventurous gal and I an awkward parade of an unconventional guy.'

Stopped Feeling

The sun doesn't seem to radiate on my skin the way it used to.

The absent feeling of sunlight is almost as painful as missing you.

I've given up on trying to think of what you would think of me now.

It's hard to imagine what you would look like; I'm still trying to comprehend you not being here and how.

If only I had the chance to live out your moments and live in your memories.

Even though we hadn't known one another, you will always be a part of me.

You faced the horror of what most people fear.

Your eyes were so blue, and your skin was so soft and clear.

Throughout my life I had trouble loving someone with all my heart.

In fear that things would just fall apart.

But with you there was a connection.

A love unbreakable by separation.

I can't see you, but I can feel you.

I hope as you look down you're smiling, as I'm trying to.

I'm no longer afraid to die, the thought almost seems healing.

My breaths are cutting shorter now, I've simply stopped feeling.

Bewitching Catastrophe

I wish that I could touch the sky I admire so often.

I wish that I could fall through the clouds that I get lost looking in.

It crosses my mind plenty-a-times, that I am not completely happy.

But who am I to measure true happiness and its max amount you see?

Who am I to question the measures and decisions of life?

Perhaps I have earned the weight on my back, the piling strife.

And oh, my Dear, how you are so greatly mistaken.

For my flaws, you have forsaken.

Forgotten and pushed away, neglected my true nature.

How could I compare to such beauty of whom I see you glance at; how could I compare to her?

I've come around to accept that this reflection that stares back at me is the one you'll always see.

You and the world around me.

The thought of loneliness has sunk into my mind.

And in a way the numbness doesn't bother me as much as you would think to find.

I used to like when I walked away that you would chase after me, but now I'm left alone, always turning my head just to check and see.

You are my Dear no longer, for we both have discovered; I'm a bewitching catastrophe.

Pleasant Sorry

My fists were clenched, and my mind was set.

She wasn't going to talk to me; that was a safe bet.

Angrily I grabbed my coat, and without looking back I slammed the door.

I flipped my hood up and shoved my hands in my pockets as the cold rain poured.

Beginning my walk through the busy city sidewalk.

Maneuvering through the people hearing the small side conversations as people talk.

I heard a young man complaining about the economy, another man hailing for a taxi.

One little girl jumping on her dad's back so she too can see, in this moment I wondered if she was thinking of me.

Our harsh words echoed through my mind, stopping in my tracks.

In this whole world of people, she is the only one that understands me entirely, as stranger's shoulders hit my back.

And in the sea of people, in the busy city.

I turned in the opposite direction, taking every rude and mean comment that passed by me.

Making my way through the crowd and to the front door.

I gently knocked on it, hoping the chances of us talking were a bit more.

The door slowly cracked open; her eyes peering to see.

As soon as she saw the door was swung open; she wrapped her arms around me.

Though the rain dropped on our heads and not even moments ago were we angry with each other.

She stayed put in my arms as I whispered, "I could never love another."

She looked up to me with tear filled eyes and quietly said "I thought you were leaving me."

Holding her even closer and kissing her head I responded, "I was blind to see, that you are the only one for me", both of us smiling once again in bliss of the most pleasant sorry.

she walked into the morning

with no one

but

her curiosity

"If there's a tally
of all the things I've said
in my life
that I'll see one day
it's sad to think
there's probably more lines for
'I'm sorry'
then
'I love you'."

Heart Break

It took me by surprise and consumed me all together.

At the escape of the harsh words off your once desiring lips my faith came down like a wandering feather.

I watched you walk away, but in my heart you hadn't gone.

None of it seemed real until you weren't there for me to call on.

The absence of your touch and the softness of your skin.

Still lingers through my senses and runs through my veins then my fingers tips, and through all over again.

At times I blame myself, but sometimes I blame none other than you.

For why am I in fault for believing such fantasies if I were told they were true?

My thoughts are preoccupied by the insecurities that linger through my mind.

They used to be pushed in the dusty corner of my thoughts, but they've come back since discovering you are not so kind.

I've been told of my strength and I've been told of my loving heart.

Despite these compliments, it's the flaws inside that tear me apart.

Love is a discouraging word now; thanks to you it is something I can't take.

Thanks to you I truly feel the pain of heart break.

"It's okay for me to feel this way.

Because I'm going to be okay someday."

Q o F

What scenes will they speak of when I can't speak anymore?

Who will be the last to see me, who was last at my door?

How will the final chapter be written, will foreshadow be in play or was it an ordinary day; was the middle well said?

Where can I meet my pleasant plot twist to give my story a good mix; I need something to ease my head?

When can I get my answers, or shall I receive them all too late?

Why must we have such a desire to tire over the questions of fate?

Scarred Stars

My love is lost, she kind of always has been.

Closed off from everything that scared her, for the world was so unfamiliar, I was the closest thing that she's let in.

She was lost in so many lines that other had written for her.

If you tell someone something so many times it begins to sink in their mind, soon then there's no previous perspective to pull back and refer.

So that was her and this was me, trying to be everything I could.

It was worth the nights when I didn't want to move, to see a glimpse through, this world of hers no one could see; sometimes I think I even understood.

I understood why she loved the stars, more than anyone.

For as a little girl she was told while she was in this world, she needed to be good if she wanted to be a star when her time was done.

I think she thought of that a lot, whether now she believed it or not; it helped her get through some nights.

It made me sad to see that she saw herself so dim when she was my only light.

The crack in her voice had been heard too many times.

Her laughter that filled my life was beginning to turn into a sometimes.

But I would never let her go; giving up on her is something I would never do.

And she would do the same, she didn't ignore me, she helped me a lot too.

Together we wandered off the path of security where everyone appeared to be, we made a place of our own.

Together, I helped her believe in the stars as she helped me forget my scars, never again we would feel alone.

I shared with her a thought I had about what's within a person.

Explaining, once you knew someone well enough you see a peek inside their soul and what it looks like, and those who belong together have a similar kind of setting, once I caught my breath she smiled when I was done.

I smiled with her too, for in this moment now I truly believe I could see within her.

A warm, drawing comfort that called you to strangers, a hazy little diner.

Though I haven't completely figured mine out I had the same feeling.

Tipped over mugs and coffee stains, a place to hide out when it rains, perhaps each other's little places were each other's method of healing.

When I was sad, she had a cup of coffee ready for me.

And when she felt she needed to hide I was right by her side, a safe place to be.

My love may be lost, but she won't always be.

The world's darkness will lift from her eyes one day and I can't wait for the wonders she'll see.

Until then I will read to her everything she is, not what people write on her.

And she will begin to smile again; our cups of coffee together will be the start of the love she can refer.

CHAPTER II.

"The morning witnessed my new world

that solemnly represented leaving it behind."